Contents

Introduction

Rice is the staple food for a third of the world's population and is produced in more than 100 countries. Popular world-wide, rice features in the cooking of countries as diverse as China, India, South America, Spain, Portugal, Italy and Africa. It is important to know about the varieties, so you can choose the appropriate cooking method. Rice surely is the ideal food – easy to store and quick to cook, nutritious and easy to digest and, above all, delicious.

MAIN RICE VARIETIES

There are many varieties and sub-varieties of rice and different kinds seem to appear on our supermarket shelves every day. The main types are:

Long-grain white rice is milled or polished to remove the outer husk, the germ and most of the bran; the rice has a long shape and a white opaque appearance. Sometimes called Patna rice, because it originally came from that part of India, long-grain rice now comes largely from Thailand and the USA. A popular all-purpose rice in the West for soups, stews, main course dishes, salads, pilafs, accompaniments and composite dishes, long-grain rice should be light and fluffy with separate grains. Cook for 15–18 minutes by the simmering or absorption method.

Easy-cook rice is parboiled (converted) long-grain white rice. Rice was first parboiled in India as a way of increasing its shelf life and hardness. Parboiling before milling forces the vitamins deeper into the grain, increasing its nutritional value and its cooking time, but only slightly, to 20–25 minutes. Cook by the same methods as long-grain white rice; it is more golden than long-grain white rice.

Long-grain brown rice is a slightly less refined variety, which has been milled only to remove the inedible husk. Long-grain brown rice has a distinctly nutty flavour and a much chewier texture. A soft brown colour, it is less fluffy than long-grain white rice; it is also available in an easy-cook variety. Brown rice takes slightly longer than white rice to cook, 35–40 minutes, but can be substituted for white rice in most recipes; it is especially good in salads as it has a firmer texture.

Basmati rice is sometimes called the Champagne or king of rice. This long-grain rice grown in India and Pakistan has a distinctive perfume essential in Indian pilafs and biriyanis. It has a very white colour and a slimmer grain, and is very light and fluffy when cooked. It can be used as long-grain white rice, but takes less time to cook – 10–12 minutes by the simmering or absorption method. Basmati is now available as easy-cook, but takes slightly longer to cook, 18–20 minutes. Brown Basmati Rice is unpolished and only has the husk removed. More nutritious, dense, chewy and aromatic, it takes a bit longer to cook, 45–50 minutes. Storage time is limited as the natural oils can become rancid.

Italian risotto rice is a superb medium-short-grain Italian rice used almost exclusively for creamy risottos. The rice, grown in Northern Italy, has a visible chalky line down the centre. The higher the quality, the more liquid it absorbs; up to three or four times its own volume. When cooked, it forms a creamy soupy sauce with separate grains which maintain a 'firm to the bite' texture. Look for arborio, carnaroli, roma or vialone nano; 18–20 minutes for cooking but generally 25–30 minutes in a risotto.

Spanish calaspara and la bomba rice from the area near Murcia and Valencia are superb quality medium-short-grain rices grown for paella. Substitute Italian risotto rice if you cannot find it. It cooks in about 15–18 minutes, longer in paellas, 30–35 minutes.

Pudding rice or short-grain, sometimes called Carolina rice as it was grown in the southern states of North and South Carolina, is a short-grain or round-grain rice with a chalky appearance and bland flavour. The grains are moist and sticky on cooking – perfect for puddings, custards, desserts or croquettes. Now mostly exported from China and Australia, 4 tablespoons can thicken 600 ml/1 pint/2½ cups of milk.

Thai fragrant rice or jasmine rice is a savoury white long-grain rice used in Thai and South-East Asian cooking. It has a natural aromatic flavour slightly less pronounced than basmati and it is slightly soft and sticky when cooked. Cook as for basmati; with slightly longer cooking time, about 12–15 minutes.

Japanese sushi or sticky rice is an expensive, short-grain, absorbent, sticky rice, perfect for sushi where grains must stick together to hold a shape. The opaque, pearl-like grains are white and round or slightly elongated. Grown in Japan, China and Thailand, California is now producing a medium-grain version. It cooks in about 15–20 minutes by the absorption method; it is usually mixed with a rice vinegar-sugar seasoning and fanned to cool and create a shiny appearance.

Black sweet rice or black glutinous rice is a medium short-grain rice which had a dark purple-red colour. It has a rich flavour which stands up to Asian ingredients like coconut milk and palm sugar. Used in sweet dishes in Thailand, Vietnam and Cambodia, it is available in special areas of supermarkets and Asian groceries; it cooks in 25–30

WHAT'S COOKING

Rice & Risotto

Elizabeth Wolf-Cohen

This is a Parragon Book
This edition published in 2002

Parragon
Queen Street House
4 Queen Street
Bath BA1 1HE, UK

ISBN: 0-75258-537-1

Printed in China

ACKNOWLEDGEMENTS

Editorial Consultant: Felicity Jackson
Editor: Julia Canning
Photography: Colin Bowling, Paul Forrester and Stephen Brayne
Home Economist and Stylist: Mandy Phipps

All props supplied by Barbara Stewart at Surfaces.

NOTE

Cup measurements in this book are for American cups.
Tablespoons are assumed to be 15ml. Unless otherwise stated,
milk is assumed to be full fat, eggs are medium
and pepper is freshly ground black pepper.

Recipes using uncooked eggs should be
avoided by infants, the elderly, pregnant women and anyone
suffering from an illness.

minutes by the absorption method. The colour will dye other ingredients and cookware.

Camargue red rice is a medium oval grain with a reddish brown colour found in the South of France (Carmargue is marshy land in the far south-west). It has an earthy taste and firm chewy texture. Although it loses colour in cooking, it looks good and stands up to robust flavours. Longer cooking time of 45–60 minutes by simmering or absorption method is necessary.

Wild rice, not a true rice, but an aquatic grass, is gathered by Native American Indians by canoe. This delicious nutty rice is now being cultivated; expensive, with high-quality long glossy brown-black grains, which 'flower' when fully cooked. Cook for 55–60 minutes by simmering or absorption or follow the packet instructions. As it is very expensive, it is now being sold packaged in combination with long-grain white or basmati rice. It is excellent in soups, salads, stuffings and pilafs and with full-flavoured poultry and sauces.

OTHER RICE PRODUCTS

Ground rice and rice flour is made by milling white rice to a flour-like consistency to be used as a thickener, or in cakes, pastries, cookies and puddings. Available in varying grades of coarseness from slightly granular to very fine; rice flour is generally the finest.

Rice Flakes are a form of flaked rice used in Far-Eastern cooking styles and generally function as a thickening agent, though can be deep-fat fried as a garnish.

Rice Noodles, including vermicelli, rice sticks, wide rice sticks and others are dry, rice-flour based pasta, twisted into skeins. They range in size from very fine (*sen mee*), to about 3 mm/⅛ inch thick, like tagliatelle (*sen lek*), to wide, about 1 cm/½ inch (*sen yaai*). Rehydrate in hot water for 5–20 minutes, drain and serve or use in other recipes. Some fresh rice-flour based noodles are available.

Japanese harusame noodles are very thin noodles; treat as rice vermicelli.

Vietnamese rice paper wrappers are used for spring rolls, 'wraps' or other dishes. Moistened by dipping briefly into water or spraying, they can be eaten as is, steamed or fried. They are available in various shapes and sizes.

Rice paper is an edible paper made from rice-like plants. Use it in baking to prevent sticking for foods like meringues and delicate biscuits (cookies); very thin and brittle.

Rice vinegars are red, clear, yellow or black. Wine-based, they are used in salad dressings, dipping sauces, stir-fries and other rice dishes like sushi. Flavours range from mellow to rich and fruity. Japanese vinegar is milder than Chinese. Mirin is a Japanese sweetened rice wine. Sake, Japanese rice wine, has a distinctive flavour; sherry can be used as a substitute.

COOKING METHODS

Cooking rice is not difficult, but it is important to choose the right rice for your recipe; the cooking method depends on the type of rice. As a rough guide allow 2 tablespoons of raw brown rice per serving, and 50 g/2 oz/¼ cup for other varieties; pudding recipes will vary. Two of the most basic ways of cooking rice are as follows:

Simmering is the easiest method, but imparts the least flavour. Bring a saucepan of water to the boil. Add a pinch of salt, then sprinkle in the rice and return to the boil. Reduce the heat to medium and simmer for 15–18 minutes for long-grain white rice, 20–25 minutes for easy-cook and 35–40 minutes for brown rice. Basmati rice takes less cooking time, about 10–12 minutes.

Absorption Method that the exact amount of liquid that the rice will absorb to be tender. Put the measured rice in a heavy-based saucepan, add a pinch of salt, a tablespoon of oil (optional) and 1½ times the amount of cold water. Bring to the boil over high heat; then reduce the heat to as low as possible and simmer, tightly covered, until the rice is tender and the liquid has been completely absorbed (see simmering method for timings). Do not be tempted to uncover or stir during cooking time; uncovering allows the steam to escape, altering the measured amount of liquid; stirring is even worse – it can break the fragile grains of rice, releasing the starch and making sticky rice.

Remove the pan from the heat and stand for about 5 minutes, then, using a fork, fluff into a warm serving bowl. Alternatively, after removing from the heat, uncover and place a tea towel (dish cloth) or double thickness of paper towel over the rice, re-cover and stand for 5 minutes. This method allows the steam to be absorbed rather than drip back into the rice, creating a drier, fluffier rice. Many cooks like to put the rice on a 'heat-tamer' or asbestos mat to create an even more gentle heat after the rice has come to the boil. If not, you may get a crusty (not burnt) layer of rice stuck to the bottom of the pan. However, in many cultures, this is the best bit – to loosen the crusty layer, place the pan on a wet towel for 5 minutes, then serve, or deep-fry it and serve as a snack!

Pilaf Method In a heavy-based saucepan over medium-high heat, heat two tablespoons of oil or butter and gently cook a finely chopped onion or 2–3 shallots. Add the measured rice and cook, stirring frequently until the rice is well coated with the fat and is translucent. Add 1½ times stock or water, a pinch of salt, and bring to the boil, stirring once or twice. At this point, cover the surface of the rice with a round of non-stick baking parchment or foil (to prevent the liquid from evaporating too quickly) and cover tightly; reduce the heat to as low as possible. Cooking times are as for the simmering method.

Soups & Salads

Rice not only makes soups and salads more substantial, but also adds an interesting texture and flavour to the dishes.

In the following pages you will find a variety of delicious soups using rice, from the classic Risi e Bisi, flavoured with peas, parsley and Parmesan, to a hearty Chicken & Sausage Gumbo. In Barley & Brown Rice Soup, the rice adds a nutty flavour and creates a deliciously thick consistency, turning it into a warming lunch dish. Pumpkin soup has a deliciously sweet flavour which is subtly enhanced by rice, while in Prawn Bisque with Rice, rice is used as a thickener without overpowering the delicate flavour of the soup. Soups like Vietnamese Beef & Rice Noodle Soup feature rice in the form of light, delicate noodles, while a chowder is given a different twist with wild rice and smoked chicken.

On the salad front, the nutty flavour and chewy texture of wild rice work well with the smoky flavours in Wild Rice & Bacon Salad with Scallops, and add an interesting dimension to a fruity bean salsa. Red rice from the Carmargue in the South of France also has a particular nutty flavour, which is good with the spiciness of Red Rice Salad with Hot Dressing.

You can also use rice to give old favourites a lift – try green salad with toasted rice, or turn a Greek salad into a substantial meal by adding cooked rice. Gazpacho Rice Salad is just as refreshing as the classic Spanish soup it is based on, while Caesar Salad is given an exotic touch with Thai flavourings and a rice paper garnish.

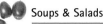

Risi e Bisi

*This famous Venetian rice soup makes an excellent substantial first course.
It should be thick but not as thick as a risotto.*

Serves 4

INGREDIENTS

900 g/2 lb fresh unshelled peas
60 g/2 oz/4 tbsp unsalted butter
1 onion, finely chopped
850 ml/1½ pints/3¾ cups chicken
   stock
200 g/7 oz/1 cup arborio rice

2 tbsp chopped fresh flat-leaf parsley
60 g/2 oz/²/₃ cup freshly grated
   Parmesan cheese
salt and pepper

TO GARNISH:
tomato slices
Parmesan cheese shavings
fresh basil leaves

1 Remove the peas from their shells – the shelled peas should weigh about 300 g/10½ oz.

2 Melt the butter in a large heavy-based saucepan over a medium heat. Add the onion and cook for about 2 minutes, stirring occasionally, until beginning to soften.

3 Add the shelled peas and cook, stirring occasionally, for a further 2–3 minutes. Gradually add the chicken stock and bring to the boil. Reduce the heat and simmer, covered, for about 10 minutes, stirring occasionally.

4 Add the rice and season with a little salt and pepper. Simmer, covered, for about 15 minutes, stirring occasionally, until the rice is just tender.

5 Stir in the parsley and adjust the seasoning. If the soup is too thick, add a little more stock. Stir in the Parmesan, then ladle into bowls.

6 Serve immediately, garnished with tomato slices, Parmesan shavings and basil leaves.

COOK'S TIP

*You can substitute 300 g/
10½ oz frozen peas for
fresh: defrost under
running hot water, add to
the softened onions and cook for
about 5 minutes with the stock.
Continue from Step 4.*

Provençal Pumpkin Winter Soup

This sweet-tasting winter soup is found throughout Provence. Sometimes thickened with potatoes or even bread, this soup uses a round rice for extra sweetness and thickening.

Serves 6

INGREDIENTS

1 kg/2 lb 4 oz fresh orange-fleshed pumpkin or winter squash, such as butternut or hubbard
2 tbsp olive oil
1 large onion, chopped
2 garlic cloves, chopped
2 tsp fresh thyme leaves

1.5 litres/2³/₄ pints/6¼ cups chicken or vegetable stock, or water
1 bay leaf
¹/₂ tsp crushed dried chillies
100 g/3¹/₂ oz/¹/₂ cup short-grain rice, such as arborio or valencia
1 tsp salt

300 ml/10 fl oz/1¹/₄ cups single (light) cream or milk
freshly grated nutmeg
pepper
fresh thyme sprigs, to garnish
garlic croûtons, to serve (optional)

1 Remove any seeds from the pumpkin, then peel. Cut into small cubes and set aside.

2 Heat the oil in a large saucepan over a medium heat. Add the onion and cook for about 4 minutes until soft.

3 Stir in the garlic and thyme and cook for 1 minute. Stir in the pumpkin, stock, bay leaf, chillies and half the rice. Bring to the boil, skimming off any foam.

Reduce the heat to low and simmer, covered, for about 1 hour until the pumpkin is very tender.

4 Meanwhile, bring a saucepan of water to the boil. Add the salt, sprinkle in the remaining rice and simmer for about 15 minutes until tender. Drain, rinse, then drain again. Set aside.

5 Working in batches, process the pumpkin soup in a blender until smooth and strain

into a large saucepan. Add the cooked rice, cream and nutmeg to taste. Season with salt and pepper and garnish with thyme. Serve with croûtons, if wished.

COOK'S TIP

Cooking half the rice separately, then adding it to the puréed soup, gives the finished dish a little texture, but if you prefer a completely smooth soup, cook all the rice at Step 3 and blend.

Tomato & Red Rice Soup

Red rice, with its firm texture and nutty flavour, is particularly good in this soup. However, if you have difficulty in finding it, long-grain brown rice can be used instead very successfully.

Serves 4–6

INGREDIENTS

2 tbsp olive oil
1 onion, finely chopped
1 carrot, finely chopped
1 stalk celery, finely chopped
3–4 garlic cloves, finely chopped
900 g/2 lb fresh ripe tomatoes, skinned, deseeded and finely chopped (see Cook's Tip)

1 bay leaf
$\frac{1}{2}$ cinnamon stick (optional)
1 tsp fresh thyme leaves or $\frac{1}{2}$ tsp dried thyme
1 tsp dried oregano
1 tbsp brown sugar
$\frac{1}{2}$ tsp cayenne pepper, or to taste

1.5 litres/2¾ pints /6¼ cups chicken stock or water
100 g/3½ oz/½ cup red rice or long-grain brown rice
1 tbsp chopped fresh oregano leaves
salt and pepper
freshly grated Parmesan cheese, to serve

1 Heat the oil in a large saucepan over a medium heat. Add the onion, carrot and celery and cook for about 10 minutes, stirring occasionally, until very soft and beginning to colour. Stir in the garlic and cook for a further minute.

2 Add the tomatoes, bay leaf, cinnamon stick, if using, thyme, dried oregano, sugar and cayenne pepper and cook, stirring occasionally, for about 5 minutes until the tomatoes begin to cook down.

3 Add the stock and the rice and bring to the boil, skimming off any foam. Reduce the heat and simmer, covered, for about 30 minutes until the rice is tender, adding more stock if necessary.

4 Stir in the fresh oregano leaves and season with salt and pepper. Serve immediately, with Parmesan cheese for sprinkling.

COOK'S TIP

You need well-flavoured tomatoes for this soup; if unavailable, use canned Italian plum tomatoes instead, and reduce the amount of stock if the tomatoes are packed in a lot of juice.

Barley & Rice Soup with Swiss Chard

This hearty winter soup makes a warming lunch or supper when served with a crusty loaf of ciabatta.

Serves 4–6

INGREDIENTS

100 g/3½ oz/½ cup pearl barley
100 g/3½ oz/½ cup long-grain brown rice
450 g/1 lb Swiss chard, trimmed and soaked for 10 minutes
2 tbsp olive oil
1 large onion, finely chopped
2 carrots, finely chopped

2 stalks celery, finely chopped
2 garlic cloves, finely chopped
400 g/14 oz can chopped Italian plum tomatoes with their juice
1 bay leaf
1 tsp dried thyme
1 tsp *herbes de Provence* or dried oregano

1 litre/1¾ pints/4 cups chicken or vegetable stock
450 g/1 lb can cannellini beans, drained
2 tbsp chopped fresh parsley
salt and pepper
freshly grated Parmesan cheese, to serve

1 Bring a large saucepan of water to the boil. Add the barley and the brown rice and return to the boil. Reduce the heat and simmer gently for 30–35 minutes until just tender. Drain and set aside.

2 Drain the Swiss chard. Cut out the hard white stems and slice the stems crossways into very thin strips; set aside. Roll the leaves into a long cigar shape and shred thinly; set aside.

3 Heat the oil in a large saucepan. Add the onion, carrots and celery and cook, stirring frequently, for about 5 minutes until soft and beginning to colour. Add the garlic and cook for a minute longer. Add the tomatoes and their juice, the bay leaf, thyme and *herbes de Provence*. Reduce the heat and simmer, partially covered, for about 7 minutes until all the vegetables are soft.

4 Stir in the sliced white chard stems and the stock. Simmer gently for about 20 minutes. Add the shredded green chard and simmer for a further 15 minutes.

5 Stir in the beans and parsley with the cooked barley and brown rice. Season with salt and pepper. Bring back to the boil and simmer for a further 8-10 minutes. Serve immediately, with Parmesan for sprinkling.

Prawn Bisque with Rice

A bisque is a shellfish soup enriched with cream and, because of the delicate flavours,
it is traditionally thickened with rice. Using basmati rice adds a slightly exotic scent.

Serves 6

INGREDIENTS

650 g/1 lb 6 oz cooked prawns
  (shrimp), in their shell
1 stalk celery, with leaves if possible,
  chopped
½ tsp crushed dried chillies
about 1.2 litres/2 pints/5 cups water
60 g/2 oz/4 tbsp butter

1 onion, finely chopped
2 carrots, finely chopped
50 ml/2 fl oz/¼ cup brandy or cognac
225 ml/8 fl oz/1 cup dry white wine
1 bay leaf and 10 parsley sprigs, tied
  together with kitchen string
1–2 tsp tomato purée (paste)

1 tsp paprika
3 tbsp basmati or long-grain white
  rice
150 ml/5 fl oz/⅔ cup double (heavy)
  or whipping cream
fresh dill sprigs or long chives, to
  garnish

1 Peel 6 prawns (shrimp), leaving the tails intact; reserve for garnishing. Peel the remaining prawns (shrimp), reserving the shells.

2 Put all the shells in a saucepan, with the celery stalk and dried chillies. Add the water. Bring to the boil over a high heat, skimming off any foam. Reduce the heat and simmer gently for about 30 minutes. Strain and set aside.

3 Melt the butter in a large saucepan. Add the onion and carrots and cook for about 8 minutes, stirring frequently, until the vegetables are soft. Add the brandy and, standing well back, ignite with a long match. Allow the flames to die down, then stir in the wine. Boil for about 5 minutes to reduce by about half.

4 Add the reserved stock, bay leaf and parsley stem bundle, tomato purée (paste), paprika and

rice; stir. Bring to the boil, then simmer gently for 20 minutes until the rice is very tender.

5 Remove the parsley bundle. Working in batches if necessary, process the soup in a blender and strain into a clean saucepan. Stir in the cream and simmer for 2–3 minutes. Add the 6 prawns (shrimp) and heat through for a minute. Ladle into 6 bowls, arranging a prawn in each serving. Garnish and serve.

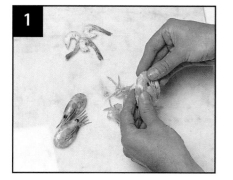

Italian Chicory & Rice Soup

This is a simple Italian soup made with the slightly bitter green scarola, or escarole, a member of the chicory family. The rice thickens the soup and gives it a delicate creaminess.

Serves 4–6

INGREDIENTS

450 g/1 lb 7 heads chicory (endive)
60 g/2 oz/4 tbsp butter
1 onion, finely chopped
1 litre/1¾ pints /4 cups chicken stock

100 g/3½ oz/½ cup arborio or
   carnaroli rice
freshly grated nutmeg

2–4 tbsp freshly grated Parmesan
   cheese
salt and pepper
fresh herbs, to garnish

1 Separate the leaves from the chicory (endive), discarding any damaged outer leaves. Wash the leaves thoroughly under cold running water and drain well. Stack several leaves in a pile and roll tightly, then shred the leaves into 1 cm/½ inch ribbons and set aside. Continue with the remaining leaves.

2 Melt the butter in a large heavy-based saucepan over a medium heat. Add the onion and cook, stirring occasionally, for about 4 minutes until soft and just beginning to colour. Stir in the shredded chicory (endive) and cook, stirring frequently, for 2 minutes until the leaves wilt.

3 Add half the stock and season with salt and pepper. Reduce the heat and simmer, covered, over a very low heat for 25–35 minutes until tender.

4 Add the remaining stock, and bring to the boil. Sprinkle in the rice and simmer, partially covered, over a medium heat for 15–20 minutes, stirring occasionally, until the rice is just tender, yet firm to the bite.

5 Remove from the heat and season with more salt and pepper, if necessary, and nutmeg. Ladle into bowls and sprinkle with a little Parmesan. Serve immediately, garnished with herbs.

COOK'S TIP

Long-grain white rice can be substituted for arborio or carnaroli, but the round rice is slightly more starchy.

Turkey & Rice Soup

You can always use the leftover turkey from Christmas or Thanksgiving to make the stock for this rich and satisfying soup.

Serves 8–10

INGREDIENTS

1 onion, finely chopped
2 carrots, diced
200 g/7 oz/1 cup long-grain white rice
2 leeks, thinly sliced
225 g/8 oz/1½ cups frozen peas
115 g/4 oz fresh or frozen (defrosted)
  mangetout (snow peas), thinly sliced
115 g/4 oz fresh spinach or watercress,
  washed and shredded

450 g/1 lb cooked turkey meat, diced
1 tbsp finely chopped fresh parsley
salt and pepper

STOCK:
1 bunch fresh parsley
2 turkey legs
1 bay leaf
1 tsp dried thyme

2 onions, unpeeled, cut into quarters
2 carrots, cut into chunks
2 stalks celery, cut into chunks
1 parsnip, cut into chunks (optional)
1 dessert apple or pear (optional)
1 tbsp black peppercorns

1 To make the stock, first tie the parsley sprigs into a bundle, then put in a large pan with the remaining stock ingredients and enough cold water to cover by 2.5 cm/1 inch.

2 Bring to the boil, over a high heat, skimming off any foam. Boil for 2 minutes, then reduce the heat to low and simmer very gently for 2–3 hours. Cool the stock slightly, then strain into a large bowl. Skim off any fat from the surface, then wipe a paper towel across the surface.

3 Put about 3 litres/5¼ pints/12 cups of the turkey stock in a large saucepan. Add the onion and carrots and bring to the boil.

4 Add the rice, reduce the heat and simmer for 15–20 minutes until the rice is tender, stirring once or twice.

5 Stir the remaining vegetables into the pan of soup and simmer for 10 minutes. Add the cooked turkey meat, heat through and season with salt and pepper. Stir in the parsley and serve.

Wild Rice & Smoked Chicken Chowder

Adding wild rice to soups gives wonderful texture as well as flavour – and it looks good too. The smoky flavour of the chicken complements the nuttiness of the wild rice.

Serves 6–8

INGREDIENTS

75 g/2¾ oz/½ cup wild rice, washed
3 fresh corn-on-the-cobs, husks and
   silks removed
2 tbsp vegetable oil
1 large onion, finely chopped
1 stalk celery, thinly sliced

1 leek, trimmed and thinly sliced
½ tsp dried thyme
2 tbsp plain (all-purpose) flour
1 litre/1¾ pints /4 cups chicken stock
250 g/9 oz boned smoked chicken,
   skinned, diced or shredded

225 ml/8 fl oz/1 cup double (heavy) or
   whipping cream
1 tbsp chopped fresh dill
salt and pepper
fresh dill sprigs, to garnish

1 Bring a large saucepan of water to the boil. Add a tablespoon of salt and sprinkle in the wild rice. Return to the boil, then reduce the heat and simmer, covered, for about 40 minutes until just tender, but still firm to the bite. Do not overcook the rice as it will continue to cook in the soup. Drain and rinse; set aside.

2 Hold the corn cobs vertical to a cutting board and, using a sharp heavy knife, cut down along the cobs to remove the kernels.

Set aside the kernels. Scrape the cob to remove the milky juices; reserve for the soup.

3 Heat the oil in a large pan over a medium heat. Add the onion, celery, leek and dried thyme. Cook, stirring frequently, for about 8 minutes until the vegetables are very soft.

4 Sprinkle over the flour and stir until blended. Gradually whisk in the stock, add the corn with any juices and bring to the boil; skim off any foam. Reduce the heat and simmer for about 25 minutes until the vegetables are very soft and tender.

5 Stir in the smoked chicken, wild rice, cream and dill. Season with salt and pepper. Simmer for 10 minutes until the chicken and rice are heated through. Garnish with dill sprigs and serve immediately.

Chicken & Sausage Gumbo

This is the nearest you can get to a true gumbo living outside 'Cajun country'.
Gumbos are always served around a dome of white rice.

Serves 6–8

INGREDIENTS

1.25 kg/2 lb 12 oz chicken, cut into 8 pieces

85 g/3¼ oz/¾ cup plain (all-purpose) flour

175 ml/6 fl oz/¾ cup vegetable oil

700 g/1 lb 9 oz andouille (Cajun smoked sausage), Polish kielbasa or other smoked pork sausage, cut into 5 cm/2 inch pieces

2 large onions, finely chopped

3–4 stalks celery, finely chopped

2 green (bell) peppers, deseeded and finely chopped

700 g/1 lb 9 oz okra, stems trimmed and cut into 1 cm/½ inch pieces

4 garlic cloves, finely chopped

2 bay leaves

½ tsp cayenne pepper, or to taste

1 tsp ground black pepper

1 tsp any dry mustard powder

1 tsp dried thyme

½ tsp ground cumin

½ tsp dried oregano

1.5 litres/2¾ pints /6¼ cups chicken stock, simmering

3–4 ripe tomatoes, deseeded and chopped

salt

400 g/14 oz/2 cups long-grain white rice, cooked, to serve

1 Toss the chicken in about 2 tablespoons of the flour. Heat 2 tablespoons of the oil in a large frying pan (skillet). Add the chicken and cook for about 10 minutes until golden. Set aside.

2 Add the sausage pieces to the pan, stirring and tossing, for about 5 minutes until beginning to colour. Set aside.

3 Heat the remaining oil in the cleaned-out pan until just beginning to smoke. Add the remaining flour all at once and whisk immediately to blend into the oil. Reduce the heat and cook, stirring, for about 20 minutes until the roux is a deep rich brown.

4 Add the onions, celery and (bell) peppers to the roux and cook, stirring frequently, for about 3 minutes until beginning to soften. Stir in the okra, garlic, bay leaves, cayenne pepper, black pepper, mustard powder, thyme, cumin and oregano and stir well.

5 Little by little, whisk the hot stock into the mixture, stirring well after each addition. Simmer for about 10 minutes. Stir in the tomatoes and the reserved sausage and chicken pieces and simmer for about 20 minutes until the meat is tender.

6 To serve, fill a cup with rice, packing it lightly, then unmould into the centre of a wide soup bowl. Spoon the gumbo around the rice.

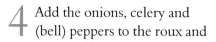

Vietnamese Beef & Rice Noodle Soup

Exotic flavours combine with French finesse in this exquisitely delicious main course soup, called 'pho' in Vietnam. If you can, make the stock a day in advance for the best flavour.

Serves 4–6

INGREDIENTS

175 g/6 oz packet dried rice stick
   noodles
4–6 spring onions (scallions), sliced
   thinly on the diagonal
1 fresh red chilli, sliced thinly on the
   diagonal
1 bunch fresh coriander (cilantro)

1 bunch fresh mint
350 g/12 oz fillet or rib eye steak, very
   thinly sliced
salt and pepper

STOCK:
900 g/2 lb meaty beef bones
4 spring onions (scallions), chopped
2 carrots, cut into chunks
1 leek, cut into chunks
3 whole star anise
1 tsp black peppercorns

1 To make the stock, put the beef bones, spring onions (scallions), carrots, leek, star anise and peppercorns in a large saucepan or flameproof casserole and bring to the boil, skimming off any foam. Reduce the heat and simmer gently, partially covered, for about 3 hours.

2 Strain into a large bowl and skim off any fat; draw a paper towel across the surface to remove any drops of fat.

3 Cover the noodles with warm water and leave for about 3 minutes until just softened; drain the noodles. Using scissors, snip the noodles into 10 cm/4 inch lengths.

4 Arrange the spring onions (scallions) and chilli on a serving plate. Strip the leaves from the coriander (cilantro) stems and arrange in a pile on the plate. Strip the leaves from the mint stems and arrange in a pile next to the coriander (cilantro) leaves.

5 Bring the beef stock to the boil in a large saucepan. Add the noodles and simmer for about 2 minutes until tender. Add the beef strips and simmer for about 1 minute. Season to taste.

6 Ladle the soup into bowls and serve with the spring onions (scallions), chilli and herbs handed separately.

Warm Greek-style Rice Salad

This easy-to-make rice salad has all the flavours of the Aegean – olive oil, lemon, feta cheese, capers and tomatoes. It is ideal as an accompaniment to barbecued lamb or chicken.

Serves 4–6

INGREDIENTS

200 g/7 oz/1 cup long-grain white rice
80 ml/3 fl oz/¹⁄₃ cup extra-virgin olive oil
2–3 tbsp lemon juice
1 tbsp chopped fresh oregano or 1 tsp dried oregano
¹⁄₂ tsp Dijon mustard

2 large ripe tomatoes, deseeded and chopped
1 red or green (bell) pepper, deseeded and chopped
75 g/2³⁄₄ oz Kalamata or other brine-cured black olives, stoned (pitted) and halved

225 g/8 oz feta cheese, crumbled, plus extra cubes, to garnish
1 tbsp capers, rinsed and drained
2–4 tbsp chopped fresh flat-leaf parsley or coriander (cilantro)
salt and pepper
diced cucumber, to garnish

1 Bring a saucepan of water to the boil. Add a teaspoon of salt and sprinkle in the rice; return to the boil, stirring once or twice. Reduce the heat and simmer for 15–20 minutes until the rice is tender, stirring once or twice. Drain and rinse under hot running water; drain again.

2 Meanwhile, whisk together the olive oil, lemon juice, oregano, mustard and salt and pepper in a bowl. Add the tomatoes, (bell) pepper, olives, feta cheese, capers and parsley and stir to coat in the dressing. Leave to marinate.

3 Turn the rice into a large bowl; add to the vegetable mixture and toss to mix well.

4 Season the salad with salt and pepper to taste, then divide between 4–6 individual dishes and garnish with extra feta cheese cubes and diced cucumber. Serve just warm.

VARIATION

This salad is also delicious made with brown rice – just increase the cooking time to 25–30 minutes.

Wild Rice & Bacon Salad with Scallops

Wild rice has a nutty, slightly chewy texture, which is great in salads.
The smokiness of the bacon and the sweetness of the scallops make a perfect combination.

Serves 4

INGREDIENTS

150 g/5¹/₂ oz/1 cup wild rice
600 ml/1 pint/2¹/₂ cups water or more
  if necessary
50 g/1³/₄ oz/¹/₂ cup pecans or walnuts
2 tbsp vegetable oil

4 slices smoked bacon, diced or sliced
3–4 shallots, finely chopped
80 ml/3 fl oz/¹/₃ cup walnut oil
2–3 tbsp sherry or cider vinegar
2 tbsp chopped fresh dill

8–12 large scallops, cut lengthways
  in half
salt and pepper
lemon and lime slices, to serve

1 Put the wild rice in a saucepan with the water and bring to the boil, stirring once or twice. Reduce the heat to low, cover, and simmer gently for 30–50 minutes, depending on whether you prefer a chewy or tender texture. Using a fork, fluff the rice into a large bowl; allow to cool slightly.

2 Meanwhile, toast the nuts in a frying pan (skillet) for 2–3 minutes until just beginning to colour, stirring frequently. Cool and chop coarsely; set aside.

3 Heat a tablespoon of the vegetable oil in the pan. Stir in the bacon and cook, stirring occasionally, until crisp and brown. Transfer to paper towels to drain. Remove some of the oil from the pan and stir in the shallots. Cook for 3–4 minutes, stirring from time to time, until soft.

4 Stir the toasted nuts, bacon and shallots into the rice. Add the walnut oil, vinegar, half the chopped dill and salt and pepper to taste. Toss well to combine the ingredients, then set aside.

5 Brush a large non-stick frying pan (skillet) with the remaining oil. Heat until very hot, add the scallops and cook for 1 minute on each side until golden; do not overcook.

6 Divide the wild rice salad among 4 individual plates. Top with the scallops and sprinkle with the remaining dill. Garnish with a sprig of dill, if desired and serve immediately with the lemon and lime slices.

Spicy Rice, Bean & Corn Salad

This hearty rice salad was inspired by the famous American dish called succatash. It is easy to put together and makes a great addition to a summer barbecue or grilled (broiled) chicken or pork.

Serves 4–6

INGREDIENTS

100 g/3¹/₂ oz/¹/₂ cup long-grain white or brown rice

3 corn-on-the-cobs

groundnut oil

1 small red onion, finely chopped

1 fresh red or green chilli, deseeded and finely chopped

1 tbsp lemon juice

1 tbsp lime juice

¹/₂ tsp cayenne pepper, or to taste

2 tbsp chopped fresh coriander (cilantro)

400 g/14 oz can butter beans

115 g/4 oz sliced cooked ham, diced

salt and pepper

1 Bring a saucepan of water to the boil. Add a teaspoon of salt and sprinkle in the rice. Return to the boil, stirring once or twice. Reduce the heat and simmer for 15–20 minutes until the rice is tender. (Brown rice will take 25–30 minutes.) Drain and rinse under cold running water; drain and set aside.

2 Scrape down each corn cob with a knife to remove the kernels; set aside. Scrape along each cob to remove the milky residue and transfer to a small bowl.

3 Heat 1 tablespoon of the oil in a saucepan. Add the corn kernels and cook gently for about 5 minutes, stirring frequently, until tender. Add the red onion and chilli and stir for about 1 minute until blended. Transfer to a plate and allow to cool slightly.

4 Place the lemon and lime juices in a large bowl and whisk in the cayenne pepper, 2–3 tablespoons of oil and the milky corn liquid. Whisk in the chopped coriander (cilantro) until well combined.

5 Using a fork, fluff in the cooked rice and corn and onion mixture. Add the beans and ham and season with salt and pepper. Transfer to a serving bowl and serve immediately.

COOK'S TIP

Although fresh corn-on-the-cob has a delicious flavour, you could substitute canned or defrosted frozen corn kernels without any problem.

Gazpacho Rice Salad

This rice salad has all the flavours of a zesty Spanish gazpacho. Garlic, tomatoes, (bell) peppers and cucumber combined with rice make a great summer salad.

Serves 4–6

INGREDIENTS

extra-virgin olive oil
1 onion, finely chopped
4 garlic cloves, finely chopped
200 g/7 oz/1 cup long-grain white rice or basmati
350 ml/12 fl oz/1¹/₂ cups vegetable stock or water
1¹/₂ tsp dried thyme
3 tbsp sherry vinegar
1 tsp Dijon mustard

1 tsp honey or sugar
1 red (bell) pepper, cored, deseeded and chopped
¹/₂ yellow (bell) pepper, cored, deseeded and chopped
¹/₂ green (bell) pepper, cored, deseeded and chopped
1 red onion, finely chopped
¹/₂ cucumber, peeled, deseeded and chopped (optional)

3 tomatoes, deseeded and chopped
2–3 tbsp chopped flat-leaf parsley
salt and pepper

TO SERVE:
12 cherry tomatoes, halved
12 black olives, stoned (pitted) and coarsely chopped
1 tbsp flaked (slivered) almonds, toasted

1 Heat 2 tablespoons of the oil in a large saucepan. Add the onion and cook for 2 minutes, stirring frequently, until beginning to soften. Stir in half the garlic and cook for a further minute.

2 Add the rice, stirring well to coat, and cook for about 2 minutes until translucent. Stir in the stock and half the thyme and

bring to the boil; season with salt and pepper. Simmer very gently, covered, for about 20 minutes until tender. Stand, still covered, for about 15 minutes; uncover and cool completely.

3 Whisk the vinegar with the remaining garlic and thyme, the mustard, honey and salt and pepper in a large bowl. Slowly

whisk in about 80 ml/3 fl oz/¹/₃ cup of the olive oil. Using a fork, fluff the rice into the vinaigrette.

4 Add the (bell) peppers, red onion, cucumber, tomatoes and parsley; toss and season.

5 Transfer to a serving bowl and garnish with the tomatoes, olives and almonds. Serve warm.

Thai-style Caesar Salad

This simple salad uses fried rice paper wrappers as crispy croûtons on a simple salad of cos (romaine) leaves. The Thai fish sauce gives the dressing an unusual flavour.

Serves 4

INGREDIENTS

1 large head cos (romaine) lettuce, with outer leaves removed, or 2 hearts
vegetable oil, for deep frying
4–6 large rice paper wrappers or 120 g/4 oz rice paper flakes

small bunch of coriander (cilantro), leaves stripped from stems

DRESSING:
80 ml/3 fl oz/⅓ cup rice vinegar
2–3 tbsp Thai fish sauce

2 garlic cloves, coarsely chopped
1 tbsp sugar
2.5 cm/1 inch piece fresh ginger root, peeled and coarsely chopped
120 ml/4 fl oz/½ cup sunflower oil
salt and pepper

1 Tear the lettuce leaves into bite-sized pieces and put into a large salad bowl.

2 To make the dressing, put the vinegar, fish sauce, garlic, sugar and ginger in a food processor and process for 15–30 seconds.

3 With the machine running, gradually pour in the sunflower oil until a creamy liquid forms. Season with salt and pepper and pour into a jug; set aside.

4 Heat about 7.5 cm/3 inches of vegetable oil in a deep-fat fryer to 190°C/375°F.

5 Meanwhile, break the rice wrappers into bite-sized pieces and dip each into a bowl of water to soften. Lay on a clean tea towel (dish cloth) and pat completely dry.

6 Working in batches, add the rice paper pieces to the hot oil and fry for about 15 seconds until crisp and golden. Using a slotted spoon, transfer to paper towels to drain.

7 Add the coriander (cilantro) leaves to the lettuce and toss to mix. Add the fried rice paper 'crisps' and drizzle over the dressing. Toss to coat the leaves and serve immediately.

VARIATION

Substitute 2 tablespoons of the sunflower oil with sesame oil for a different flavour.

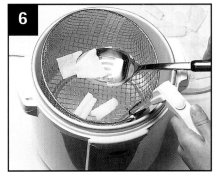

Brown Rice, Lentil & Shiitake Salad

Fresh shiitakes, which are now widely available,
give this substantial salad a good mushroomy flavour.

Serves 6–8

INGREDIENTS

225 g/8 oz/1 cup Puy lentils, rinsed
4 tbsp olive oil
1 onion, finely chopped
200 g/7 oz/1 cup long-grain brown
　rice
1/2 tsp dried thyme
450 ml/16 fl oz/2 cups chicken stock
350 g/12 oz shiitake mushrooms,
　trimmed and sliced

2 garlic cloves, finely chopped
115 g/4 oz smoked bacon, diced and
　fried until crisp
2 small courgettes (zucchini), diced
1–2 stalks celery, thinly sliced
6 spring onions (scallions), thinly sliced
2–3 tbsp chopped fresh flat-leaf parsley
2 tbsp walnut halves, toasted and
　coarsely chopped

salt and pepper

DRESSING:
2 tbsp red or white wine vinegar
1 tbsp balsamic vinegar
1 tsp Dijon mustard
1 tsp sugar
80 ml/3 fl oz/1/3 cup extra-virgin olive oil
2–3 tbsp walnut oil

1 Bring a large saucepan of water to the boil. Add the lentils, bring back to the boil, then simmer for about 30 minutes until just tender; do not overcook. Drain and rinse under cold running water; drain and set aside.

2 Heat 2 tablespoons of the oil in a large saucepan. Add the onion and cook until it begins to soften. Add the rice; stir to coat.

Add the thyme, stock and salt and pepper; bring to the boil. Simmer very gently, covered tightly, for about 40 minutes until the rice is tender and the liquid absorbed.

3 Heat the remaining oil in a frying pan (skillet) and stir-fry the mushrooms for about 5 minutes until golden. Stir in the garlic and cook for a further 30 seconds. Season with salt and pepper.

4 To make the dressing, whisk together the vinegars, mustard and sugar in a large bowl. Gradually whisk in the oils. Season with salt and pepper. Add the lentils and gently toss. Fork in the rice. Toss.

5 Stir in the bacon and mushrooms, then courgettes (zucchini), celery, spring onions (scallions) and parsley and season. Serve sprinkled with walnuts.

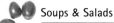

Moroccan Mixed Rice Salad

The combination of spices gives this rice salad a slightly exotic scent.
Toasting the spices mellows the harshness and brings out their flavours.

Serves 4–6

INGREDIENTS

800 ml/1¹/₃ pints/3¹/₂ cups water
1 tbsp soy sauce
1 tbsp unsulphured molasses
75 g/2³/₄ oz/¹/₂ cup wild rice
2 tbsp olive oil
100 g/3¹/₂ oz/¹/₂ cup long-grain brown
  or white rice
425 g/15 oz can chick peas (garbanzo
  beans), rinsed and drained
¹/₂ red onion, finely chopped

1 small red (bell) pepper, deseeded
  and diced
80 g/3 oz ready-soaked dried
  apricots, sliced
75 g/2³/₄ oz/¹/₂ cup raisins
2 tbsp chopped fresh mint or
  coriander (cilantro)
60 g/2 oz/scant ¹/₂ cup flaked (slivered)
  almonds, toasted
lettuce leaves, to garnish
lemon wedges, to serve

SPICED DRESSING:
1 tsp hot curry powder
1 tsp ground coriander
1 tsp ground turmeric
1 tsp freshly ground nutmeg
¹/₂ tsp cayenne pepper
50 ml/2 fl oz/¹/₄ cup rice vinegar
2 tbsp honey
1 tbsp lemon juice
80 ml/3 fl oz/¹/₃ cup extra-virgin
  olive oil

1 Put 350 ml/12 fl oz/1½ cups of the water, the soy sauce and molasses in a saucepan and bring to the boil. Add the wild rice and bring back to the boil. Cover and simmer gently for 30–50 minutes depending on whether you prefer a chewy or tender texture. Remove from the heat to cool slightly.

2 Heat the oil in a saucepan, add the brown rice and stir for about 2 minutes to coat with the oil. Add the remaining water and bring to the boil; reduce the heat to low and simmer, covered tightly, for about 40 minutes until the rice is tender and all the water is absorbed. Remove from the heat to cool slightly.

3 Meanwhile, make the dressing; put the ground spices in a small frying pan (skillet) and cook gently for 4–5 minutes, stirring, until golden. Cool on a small plate. Whisk together the vinegar, honey and lemon juice in a large bowl, then whisk in the oil, until the dressing thickens. Whisk in the cooled spice mixture.

4 Fork the brown rice and wild rice into the dressing and mix well. Stir in the chick peas (garbanzo beans), onion, (bell) pepper, apricots, raisins and mint.

5 To serve, sprinkle with the almonds, garnish with lettuce and serve with lemon wedges.

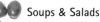
Pesto Risotto-rice Salad

This is a cross between a risotto and a rice salad – using Italian arborio rice produces a slightly heavier, stickier result. Substituting long-grain white rice will make a lighter fluffier salad.

Serves 4–6

INGREDIENTS

extra-virgin olive oil
1 onion, finely chopped
200 g/7 oz/1 cup arborio rice
450 ml/16 fl oz/2 cups boiling water
6 sun-dried tomatoes, cut into thin
   slivers
1/2 small red onion, very thinly sliced
3 tbsp lemon juice

PESTO:
50 g/2 oz lightly packed fresh basil
   leaves
2 garlic cloves, finely chopped
2 tbsp pine kernels (nuts), lightly
   toasted
120 ml/4 fl oz/1/2 cup extra-virgin
   olive oil

50 g/1 3/4 oz/1/2 cup freshly grated
   Parmesan cheese
salt and pepper

TO GARNISH:
fresh basil leaves
Parmesan shavings

1 To make the pesto, put the basil, garlic and pine kernels (nuts) in a food processor and process for about 30 seconds. With the machine running, gradually pour in the olive oil through the feed tube, until a smooth paste forms. Add the cheese and pulse several times, until blended but still with some texture. Scrape the pesto into a small bowl and season with salt and pepper to taste. Set aside.

2 Heat 1 tablespoon of the oil in a saucepan. Add the onion and cook until beginning to soften. Add the rice and stir to coat. Cook, stirring occasionally, for about 2 minutes. Stir in the boiling water and salt and pepper. Cover and simmer very gently for 20 minutes until the rice is just tender and the water absorbed. Cool slightly.

3 Put the sun-dried tomatoes and sliced onion in a large bowl, add the lemon juice and about 2 tablespoons of oil. Fork in the hot rice and stir in the pesto. Toss to combine. Adjust the seasoning if necessary. Cover and cool to room temperature.

4 Fork the rice mixture into a shallow serving bowl. Drizzle with some olive oil and garnish with basil leaves and Parmesan. Serve the salad at room temperature, not chilled.

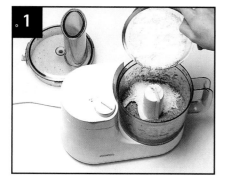

Red Rice Salad with Hot Dressing

This hearty salad is made with red rice from the Carmargue in the South of France.
It has an earthy flavour, which goes well with the other robust ingredients.

Serves 6–8

INGREDIENTS

1 tbsp olive oil
200 g/7 oz/1 cup red rice
600 ml/1 pint/2½ cups water
400 g/14 oz can red kidney beans,
   rinsed and drained
1 small red (bell) pepper, cored,
   deseeded and diced

1 small red onion, finely chopped
2 small cooked beetroots (not in
   vinegar), peeled and diced
6–8 red radishes, thinly sliced
2–3 tbsp chopped fresh chives
salt and pepper
fresh chives, to garnish

HOT DRESSING:
2 tbsp prepared horseradish
1 tbsp Dijon mustard
1 tsp sugar
50 ml/2 fl oz/¼ cup red wine vinegar
120 ml/4 fl oz/½ cup extra-virgin
   olive oil

1 Put the olive oil and red rice in a heavy-based saucepan and place over a medium heat. Add the water and 1 teaspoon of salt. Bring to the boil, reduce the heat and simmer, covered, until the rice is tender and all the water is absorbed (see Cook's Tip). Remove from the heat and allow the rice to cool to room temperature.

2 To make the dressing, put the horseradish, mustard and sugar in a small bowl and whisk to combine. Whisk in the vinegar, then gradually whisk in the oil to form a smooth dressing.

3 In a large bowl, combine the red kidney beans, red (bell) pepper, red onion, beetroot, radishes and chives and toss together. Season with salt and pepper.

4 Using a fork, fluff the rice into the bowl with the vegetables and toss together. Pour over the dressing and toss well. Cover and leave the salad to stand for about 1 hour. Spoon into a large shallow serving bowl, garnish with fresh chives and serve immediately.

COOK'S TIP

There are several red rice varieties on the market. Read the labels carefully as some require longer cooking than others.

Fruity Wild Rice Salsa with Black Beans

Wild rice has a nutty flavour and a good texture, ideal for salsas and salads. Black beans are popular in Latin-American cooking and can stand up to the strong flavours in salsas.

Serves 4–6

INGREDIENTS

150 g/5½ oz/1 cup small black beans, soaked overnight in cold water
1 onion, studded with 4 cloves
150 g/5½ oz/1 cup wild rice
2 garlic cloves, trimmed
450 ml/16 fl oz/2 cups boiling water
1 red onion, finely chopped
2 fresh red chillies, deseeded and thinly sliced

1 large red (bell) pepper, deseeded and chopped
1 small mango or papaya, peeled and diced
2 oranges, segments removed and juice reserved
4 passion fruits, pulp and juice
juice of 3–4 limes
½ tsp ground cumin

1 tbsp maple syrup or light brown sugar
150 ml/5 fl oz/⅔ cup extra-virgin olive oil
1 small bunch coriander (cilantro), leaves stripped from stems and chopped
lime slices, to garnish

1 Drain the soaked beans and put in a large saucepan with the clove-studded onion. Cover with cold water by at least 5 cm/2 inches. Bring to the boil, reduce the heat to low and simmer for 1 hour until the beans are tender. Discard the onion, rinse under cold running water, drain and set aside.

2 Meanwhile, put the wild rice and garlic in a saucepan and cover with the boiling water. Simmer, covered, over a low heat for 30–50 minutes depending on the preferred texture. Cool slightly; discard the garlic cloves.

3 Put the beans in a large bowl and fork in the wild rice. Add the onion, chillies, (bell) pepper, mango, orange segments and their juice and the passion fruit pulp and juice. Toss well together.

4 Combine the lime juice, ground cumin and maple syrup. Whisk in the olive oil and half the coriander (cilantro), then pour over the bean/rice mixture and toss well. Cover and allow the flavours to blend for up to 2 hours.

5 Spoon into a serving bowl, sprinkle with the remaining coriander (cilantro) and serve garnished with lime slices.

Prawn (Shrimp) Salad & Toasted Rice

*This simple salad is tossed with an unusual Vietnamese-style dressing
and sprinkled with dry toasted rice, which gives interesting texture and flavour.*

Serves 4

INGREDIENTS

225 g/8 oz raw cooked (shrimp), with
   tail shells left on
2 tbsp sunflower oil
cayenne pepper
1 tbsp long-grain white rice
1 large head cos (romaine) lettuce with
   outer leaves removed or 2 hearts

½ small English cucumber, lightly
   peeled, deseeded and thinly sliced
1 small bunch chives, sliced into
   2.5 cm/1 inch pieces
handful of fresh mint leaves
salt and pepper

DRESSING:
50 ml/2 fl oz/¼ cup rice vinegar
1 red chilli, deseeded and thinly sliced
7.5 cm/3 inch piece lemon grass stalk,
   crushed
juice of 1 lime
2 tbsp Thai fish sauce
1 tsp sugar, or to taste

1 Split each prawn (shrimp) in half lengthways, leaving the tail attached to one half. Remove any dark intestinal veins and pat dry. Sprinkle with a little salt and cayenne pepper.

2 To make the dressing, combine the vinegar with the chilli and lemon grass. Leave to marinate.

3 Heat a wok or heavy-based frying pan (skillet) over high heat. Add the rice and stir until brown and richly fragrant. Turn into a mortar and cool completely. Crush gently with a pestle until coarse crumbs form.

4 Stir-fry the prawns (shrimp) in the cleaned pan for 1 minute until warm. Transfer to a plate and season with pepper.

5 Tear or shred the lettuce into large bite-sized pieces and transfer to a shallow salad bowl. Add the cucumber, chives and mint leaves and toss to combine.

6 Remove the lemon grass and most of the chilli slices from the rice vinegar and whisk in the lime juice, fish sauce, water and sugar. Pour most of the dressing over the salad and toss. Top with the prawns (shrimp) and drizzle with the remaining dressing. Sprinkle with the toasted rice and serve.

Thai Noodle Salad with Prawns (Shrimp)

This delicious combination of rice noodles and prawns (shrimp), lightly dressed with typical Thai flavours, makes an impressive first course or light lunch.

Serves 4

INGREDIENTS

80 g/3 oz rice vermicelli or rice sticks

175 g/6 oz mangetout (snow peas), cut crossways in half, if large

5 tbsp lime juice

4 tbsp Thai fish sauce

1 tbsp sugar, or to taste

2.5 cm/1 inch piece fresh ginger root, peeled and finely chopped

1 fresh red chilli, deseeded and thinly sliced on the diagonal

4 tbsp chopped fresh coriander (cilantro) or mint, plus extra for garnishing

10 cm/4 inch piece of cucumber, peeled, deseeded and diced

2 spring onions (scallions), thinly sliced on the diagonal

16–20 large cooked, peeled prawns (shrimp)

2 tbsp chopped unsalted peanuts or cashews (optional)

4 whole cooked prawns (shrimp) and lemon slices, to garnish

1 Put the rice noodles in a large bowl and pour over enough hot water to cover. Stand for about 4 minutes until soft. Drain and rinse under cold running water; drain and set aside.

2 Bring a saucepan of water to the boil. Add the mangetout (snow peas) and return to the boil. Simmer for 1 minute. Drain, rinse under cold running water until cold, then drain and set aside.

3 In a large bowl, whisk together the lime juice, fish sauce, sugar, ginger, chilli and coriander (cilantro). Stir in the cucumber and spring onions (scallions). Add the drained noodles, mangetout (snow peas) and the prawns (shrimp). Toss the salad gently together.

4 Divide the noodle salad among 4 large plates. Sprinkle with chopped coriander (cilantro)

and the peanuts (if using), then garnish each plate with a whole prawn (shrimp) and a lemon slice. Serve immediately.

COOK'S TIP

There are many sizes of rice noodles available – make sure you use the very thin rice noodles, called rice vermicelli or rice sticks or sen mee, otherwise the salad will be too heavy.

Wild Rice Blini with Smoked Salmon

Blinis are small Russian pancakes made with a combination of white and buckwheat flours.
The addition of wild rice adds more texture and a nutty flavour to a real classic.

Makes about 50 blinis

INGREDIENTS

butter or oil for frying
4 spring onions (scallions), thinly
  sliced on the diagonal
115 g/4 oz smoked salmon, thinly
  sliced or shredded
120 ml /4 fl oz/¹/₂ cup soured cream
chopped chives, to garnish

BLINIS:
80 ml/3 fl oz/¹/₃ cup lukewarm water
1¹/₂ tsp dried yeast
60 g/2 oz/¹/₂ cup plain (all-purpose)
  flour
70 g/2¹/₂ oz/¹/₂ cup plus 1 tbsp
  buckwheat flour

2 tbsp sugar
¹/₂ tsp salt
225 ml/8 fl oz/1 cup milk
2 eggs, separated
25 g/1 oz/2 tbsp butter, melted
60 g/2 oz/1 cup cooked wild rice

1 Pour the lukewarm water into a small bowl and sprinkle over the yeast. Stand until the yeast has dissolved and the mixture is beginning to bubble.

2 Sift the flours into a large bowl and stir in the sugar and salt. Make a well in the centre. Warm 175 ml/6 fl oz/¾ cup milk and add to the well with the yeast mixture. Gradually whisk the flour into the liquid to form a smooth batter. Cover the bowl with cling film (plastic wrap) and leave to stand in a warm place until light and bubbly.

3 Beat the remaining milk with the egg yolks and the melted butter and beat into the batter.

4 Using an electric mixer, beat the egg whites until soft peaks form. Fold a spoonful into the batter, then fold in the remaining egg whites and the wild rice alternately; do not over mix.

5 Heat a little butter or oil in a large frying pan (skillet) to lightly coat. Drop tablespoons of the batter into the pan and cook for 1–2 minutes until tiny bubbles form on the surface. Turn and cook for 30 seconds. Remove and keep warm in a low oven while cooking the remaining batter.

6 To serve, top with the spring onions (scallions), smoked salmon strips, a dollop of soured cream and a sprinkling of chives.

Main Dishes & Accompaniments

Rice, like wheat, is one of the world's most versatile ingredients. It can be used as the focal point of a main dish or as a subtle accompaniment to roasts and stews.

Use rice as the base of a substantial dish like Chicken Basquaise, to soak up the flavours of South West France, or combine it with lamb and exotic spices to create a delicious Eastern-style pilaf, perfect for informal entertaining. Rice is ideal for making one-pot dishes – Seafood Rice, a marvellous mix of mussels, clams, peppers and chilli, proves the point, or follow the Cuban tradition of serving rice with black beans, sausage and ham for a truly satisfying dish.

Try transforming rice into curried patties, a tasty vegetarian alternative to burgers, or use rice as a foil to the strong flavours of stir-fries – the ginger fried rice dish, topped with succulent soy-glazed duck, is an oriental treat. Noodles made from rice also provide excellent all-in-one dishes – try Pad Thai with chicken and crab for an exotic supper.

Delicate flavours go well with rice, especially if the rice is used as an accompaniment. Lemon-scented Rice with Mint will enhance any dish, from a Middle-Eastern tajine to a French beef casserole, while Fragrant Orange Basmati Rice is the perfect accompaniment to steamed fish or poultry dishes.

Chicken Basquaise

Sweet (bell) peppers are a typical ingredient of dishes from the Basque region in the far West of France. In this recipe, the addition of Bayonne ham, the famous air-dried ham from the Pyrenees, adds a delicious flavour.

Serves 4–5

INGREDIENTS

1.35 kg/3 lb chicken, cut into 8 pieces
flour, for dusting
2–3 tbsp olive oil
1 large onion, (preferably Spanish),
    thickly sliced
2 (bell) peppers, deseeded and cut
    lengthways into thick strips
2 garlic cloves

150 g/5 oz spicy chorizo sausage,
    peeled, if necessary, and cut into
    1 cm/¹/₂ inch pieces
1 tbsp tomato purée (paste)
200 g/7 oz/1 cup long-grain white
    rice or medium-grain Spanish rice,
    such as valencia
450 ml/16 fl oz/2 cups chicken stock

1 tsp crushed dried chillies
¹/₂ tsp dried thyme
120 g/4 oz Bayonne or other air-dried
    ham, diced
12 dry-cured black olives
2 tbsp chopped fresh flat-leaf parsley
salt and pepper

1 Dry the chicken pieces well with paper towel. Put about 2 tablespoons flour in a plastic bag, season with salt and pepper and add the chicken pieces. Seal the bag and shake to coat the chicken.

2 Heat 2 tablespoons of the oil in a large flameproof casserole over a medium-high heat. Add the chicken and cook for about 15 minutes until well browned. Transfer to a plate.

3 Heat the remaining oil in the pan and add the onion and (bell) peppers. Reduce the heat to medium and stir-fry until beginning to colour and soften. Add the garlic, chorizo and tomato purée (paste) and continue stirring for about 3 minutes. Add the rice and cook for about 2 minutes, stirring to coat, until the rice is translucent.

4 Add the stock, crushed chillies and thyme and salt and pepper and stir. Bring to the boil. Return the chicken to the pan, pressing gently into the rice. Cover and cook over a very low heat for about 45 minutes until the chicken and rice are tender.

5 Gently stir the ham, black olives and half the parsley into the rice mixture. Re-cover and heat through for a further 5 minutes. Sprinkle with the remaining parsley and serve.

Pad Thai

All over Thailand and South-East Asia, street stalls (even floating ones!) sell these simple delicious rice noodles, stir-fried to order. Serve with a selection of traditional accompaniments.

Serves 4

INGREDIENTS

225 g/8 oz flat rice noodles (*sen lek*)
2 tbsp groundnut or vegetable oil
225 g/8 oz boneless chicken breasts, skinned and thinly sliced
4 shallots, finely chopped
2 garlic cloves, finely chopped
4 spring onions (scallions), cut on the diagonal into 5 cm/2 inch pieces
350 g/12 oz fresh white crab meat

75 g/2¾ oz/1 cup fresh bean-sprouts, rinsed
1 tbsp preserved radish or fresh radish, finely diced
2–4 tbsp roasted peanuts, chopped
fresh coriander (cilantro) sprigs, to garnish

SAUCE:
3 tbsp Thai fish sauce
2–3 tbsp rice vinegar or cider vinegar
1 tbsp chilli bean sauce or oyster sauce
1 tbsp toasted sesame oil
1 tbsp palm sugar or light brown sugar
½ tsp cayenne pepper or fresh red chilli, thinly sliced

1 To make the sauce, whisk together the sauce ingredients in a small bowl and set aside.

2 Put the rice noodles in a large bowl and pour over enough hot water to cover; leave to stand for 15 minutes until softened. Drain, rinse and drain again.

3 Heat the oil in a heavy-based wok over a high heat until very hot, but not smoking. Add the chicken strips and stir-fry for 1–2 minutes until they just begin to colour. Using a slotted spoon, transfer to a plate. Reduce the heat to medium-high.

4 Stir the shallots, garlic and spring onions (scallions) into the wok and stir-fry for about 1 minute. Stir in the drained noodles, then the prepared sauce.

5 Return the reserved chicken to the pan with the crab meat, bean-sprouts and radish; toss well. Cook for about 5 minutes until heated through, tossing frequently. If the noodles begin to stick, add a little water.

6 Turn into a serving dish and sprinkle with the chopped peanuts. Garnish with coriander (cilantro) and serve immediately.

Stir-fried Ginger Rice with Duck

For the best result, buy a 2.25 kg/5 lb duck, remove the breasts and use the carcass to make a flavourful stock, simmering it with 2 quartered onions, some peppercorns and sliced ginger root.

Serves 4–6

INGREDIENTS

2 duck breasts, cut into thin slices on the diagonal
2–3 tbsp Japanese soy sauce
1 tbsp mirin (sweet rice wine) or sherry
2 tsp brown sugar
5 cm/2 inch piece fresh ginger root, finely chopped or grated
4 tbsp peanut oil

2 garlic cloves, crushed
300 g/10¹⁄₂ oz/1¹⁄₂ cups long-grain white or brown rice
800 ml/1¹⁄₃ pints/3¹⁄₄ cups chicken stock
115 g/4 oz cooked lean ham, thinly sliced
175 g/6 oz mangetout (snow peas), cut diagonally in half

40 g/1¹⁄₂ oz/¹⁄₂ cup fresh bean-sprouts, rinsed
8 spring onions (scallions), thinly sliced on the diagonal
2–3 tbsp chopped fresh coriander (cilantro)
sweet or hot chilli sauce (optional)

1 Put the duck in a shallow bowl with a tablespoon of soy sauce, the mirin, half the brown sugar and one-third of the ginger. Stir to coat; leave to marinate at room temperature.

2 Heat 2–3 tablespoons peanut oil in a large heavy-based saucepan over a medium-high heat. Add the garlic and half the remaining ginger and stir-fry for about 1 minute until fragrant. Add

the rice and cook for about 3 minutes, stirring, until translucent and beginning to colour.

3 Add 700 ml/1¹⁄₄ pints/scant 3 cups stock and a teaspoon of soy sauce and bring to the boil. Reduce the heat to very low and simmer, covered, for 20 minutes until the rice is tender and the liquid is absorbed. Do not uncover the pan, but remove from the heat and leave to stand.

4 Heat the remaining peanut oil in a large wok. Drain the duck breast and gently stir-fry for about 3 minutes until just coloured. Add 1 tablespoon soy sauce and the rest of the sugar and cook for 1 minute; remove to a plate and keep warm.

5 Stir in the ham, mangetout (snow peas), bean-sprouts, spring onions (scallions), the remaining ginger and half the coriander (cilantro); add about 120 ml/4 fl oz/¹⁄₂ cup of the stock and stir-fry for 1 minute, or until the stock is almost reduced. Fork in the rice and toss together. Add a few drops of chilli sauce, to taste.

6 To serve, turn into a serving dish, arrange the duck on top and sprinkle with the remaining coriander (cilantro).

Azerbaijani Lamb Pilaf

*This type of dish is popular from the Balkans, through Russia and the Middle East to India.
The saffron and pomegranate juice give it an exotic air.*

Serves 4–6

INGREDIENTS

2–3 tbsp oil
650 g/1 lb 8 oz boneless lamb
   shoulder, cut into 2.5 cm/1 inch
   cubes
2 onions, coarsely chopped
1 tsp ground cumin
200 g/7 oz/1 cup arborio, long-grain
   or basmati rice

1 tbsp tomato purée (paste)
1 tsp saffron threads
100 ml/3½ fl oz/scant ½ cup
   pomegranate juice (see Cook's Tip)
850 ml/1½ pints/3¾ cups lamb or
   chicken stock, or water
115 g/4 oz dried apricots or prunes,
   ready soaked and halved

2 tbsp raisins
salt and pepper

TO SERVE:
2 tbsp chopped fresh mint
2 tbsp chopped fresh watercress

1 Heat the oil in a large flameproof casserole or wide saucepan over a high heat. Add the lamb in batches and cook for about 7 minutes, turning, until lightly browned.

2 Add the onions to the casserole, reduce the heat to medium-high and cook for about 2 minutes until beginning to soften. Add the cumin and rice and cook for about 2 minutes, stirring to coat

well, until the rice is translucent. Stir in the tomato purée (paste) and the saffron threads.

3 Add the pomegranate juice and stock and bring to the boil, stirring once or twice. Add the apricots or prunes and raisins to the casserole, then stir together. Reduce the heat to low, cover, and simmer for 20–25 minutes until the lamb and rice are tender and the liquid is absorbed.

4 To serve, sprinkle the chopped mint and watercress over the pilaf and serve from the pan.

COOK'S TIP

Pomegranate juice is available from Middle Eastern grocery stores. If you cannot find it, substitute unsweetened grape or apple juice.

Louisiana 'Dirty' Rice

This is a classic of American Southern cooking. The dish gets its name from the greyish colour of the chicken livers and gizzards; nevertheless, it is delicious.

Serves 6

INGREDIENTS

175 g/6 oz belly pork, diced or thickly sliced bacon
225 g/8 oz chicken livers, trimmed, rinsed, dried and chopped
225 g/8 oz chicken gizzards, trimmed, rinsed, dried and finely chopped
1 onion, finely chopped

1 stalk celery, finely chopped
1 green (bell) pepper, cored, deseeded and chopped
3–4 garlic cloves, finely chopped
1 tsp ground cumin
1 tsp hot red pepper sauce, or to taste
200 g/7 oz/1 cup long-grain white rice

600 ml/1 pint/2½ cups chicken stock
2–3 spring onions (scallions), sliced
2–3 tbsp chopped fresh flat-leaf parsley
salt and pepper

1 Cook the pork in a large heavy-based saucepan for about 7 minutes until it is crisp and golden. Using a slotted spoon, remove the bacon to a plate. Add the chicken livers and gizzards and cook, stirring occasionally, for about 5 minutes until tender and lightly golden. Transfer to the plate of pork.

2 Add the onion, celery and (bell) pepper to the pan and cook for about 6 minutes, stirring frequently, until the vegetables are tender. Stir in the garlic, cumin and hot pepper sauce and cook for a further 30 seconds.

3 Add the rice and cook, stirring, until translucent and well coated with the fat. Add the stock and season with salt and pepper.

4 Return the cooked bacon, chicken livers and gizzards to the pan, stirring to blend. Cover and simmer gently for 20 minutes until the rice is tender and the liquid absorbed.

5 Fork half the spring onions (scallions) and the parsley into the rice and toss gently together. Transfer to a serving dish, sprinkle with the remaining spring onions (scallions) and serve immediately.

COOK'S TIP

If you cannot find chicken gizzards, use all chicken livers. Gizzards are available in larger supermarkets or Spanish or Caribbean groceries.

Moros y Christianos

Translated as 'Black Beans and Rice', this classic Cuban recipe is a perfect party dish – hearty, tasty and easy to make ahead.

Serves 8–10

INGREDIENTS

450 g/1 lb dried small black beans,
   soaked overnight in cold water
1 tbsp vegetable or olive oil
225 g/8 oz belly pork, diced or thickly
   sliced bacon
1 large onion, chopped (preferably
   Spanish)
2 garlic cloves, finely chopped
2 ripe tomatoes, deseeded and chopped

1 tsp ground cumin
1/2 tsp dried crushed chillies, or to taste
2 fresh bay leaves or 1 dried bay leaf
1–2 tbsp dark brown sugar
2 litres/31/2 pints/8 cups chicken stock
175 g/6 oz spicy chorizo sausage,
   peeled if necessary, cut into 1 cm/
   1/2 inch slices
900 g/2 lb ham hock

200 g/7 oz/1 cup long or medium-
   grain white rice
1–2 tbsp lime juice
1–2 tbsp chopped fresh coriander
   (cilantro) (optional)
salt and pepper
lime wedges, to garnish

1 Drain the soaked beans and rinse under cold water. Heat the oil in a large flameproof casserole over a medium heat. Add the belly pork or bacon and cook for about 4 minutes until the fat is rendered and the pork is beginning to colour.

2 Add the onion, garlic and tomatoes and cook, stirring frequently, for about 10 minutes until the vegetables are soft. Stir in the cumin, crushed chillies, bay leaves and sugar.

3 Add the drained black beans and stock. Add the chorizo, then the ham hock, pushing it well down. Bring to the boil, skimming off any foam. Partially cover, reduce the heat and simmer gently for about 2 hours, stirring occasionally, until the meat and beans are tender. Remove the ham hock and cool slightly.

4 Meanwhile, bring a saucepan of water to the boil. Add a pinch of salt and sprinkle in the rice; return to the boil. Reduce the heat and simmer gently for about 20 minutes until the rice is tender. Drain, rinse and set aside.

5 Remove the meat from the ham hock bone, cutting it into pieces, and return it to the beans. Stir in the cooked rice, lime juice and half the coriander (cilantro). Adjust the seasoning.

6 Transfer to a serving bowl and sprinkle with the remaining coriander (cilantro). Garnish with the lime wedges and serve hot.

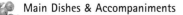

Baked Tomato Rice with Sausages

A great quick supper for the family,
this dish is incredibly simple to put together, yet is truly scrumptious!

Serves 4

INGREDIENTS

2 tbsp vegetable oil
1 onion, coarsely chopped
1 red (bell) pepper, cored, deseeded
   and chopped
2 garlic cloves, finely chopped
1/2 tsp dried thyme

300 g/10½ oz/1½ cups long-grain
   white rice
1 litre/1¾ pints/4 cups light chicken
   or vegetable stock
225 g/8 oz can chopped tomatoes
1 bay leaf
2 tbsp shredded fresh basil

175 g/6 oz mature (sharp) Cheddar
   cheese, grated
2 tbsp chopped fresh chives
4 herby pork sausages, cooked and cut
   into 1 cm/½ inch pieces
2–3 tbsp freshly grated Parmesan
   cheese

1 Heat the oil in a large flame-proof casserole over medium heat. Add the onion and red (bell) pepper and cook for about 5 minutes, stirring frequently, until soft and lightly coloured. Stir in the garlic and thyme and cook for a further minute.

2 Add the rice and cook, stirring frequently, for about 2 minutes until the rice is well coated and translucent. Stir in the stock, tomatoes and bay leaf. Boil

for 5 minutes until the stock is almost absorbed.

3 Stir in the basil, Cheddar cheese, chives and pork sausages and bake, covered, in a preheated oven at 180°C/350°F/Gas Mark 4 for about 25 minutes.

4 Sprinkle with the Parmesan cheese and return to the oven, uncovered, for 5 minutes until the top is golden. Serve hot from the casserole.

VARIATION

For a vegetarian version, replace the pork sausages with a 400 g/14 oz can of drained butter beans, kidney beans, or sweetcorn. Or try a mixture of sautéed mushrooms and courgettes (zucchini).

Seafood Rice

This satisfying rice casserole, bursting with Mediterranean flavours, can be made with any combination of seafood you choose.

Serves 4–6

INGREDIENTS

4 tbsp olive oil

16 large raw peeled prawns (shrimp), tails on if possible

225 g/8 oz cleaned squid or cuttlefish, cut into 1 cm/½ inch slices

2 green (bell) peppers, deseeded and cut lengthways into 1 cm/½ inch strips

1 large onion, finely chopped

4 garlic cloves, finely chopped

2 fresh bay leaves or 1 dried bay leaf

1 tsp saffron threads

½ tsp dried crushed chillies

400 g/14 oz/2 cups arborio or valencia rice

225 ml/8 fl oz/1 cup dry white wine

850 ml/1½ pints /3¾ cups fish, light chicken or vegetable stock

12–16 littleneck clams, well scrubbed

12–16 large mussels, well scrubbed

salt and pepper

2 tbsp chopped fresh flat-leaf parsley, to garnish

RED PEPPER SAUCE:

2–3 tbsp olive oil

2 onions, finely chopped

4–6 garlic cloves, finely chopped

4–6 Italian roasted red (bell) peppers in olive oil (not in vinegar) or roasted, peeled and coarsely chopped

420 g/14½ oz can chopped tomatoes in juice

1–1½ tsp hot paprika

salt

1 To make the red pepper sauce, heat the oil in a saucepan. Add the onions and cook for 6–8 minutes until golden. Stir in the garlic and cook for a minute. Add the remaining ingredients and simmer gently, stirring occasionally, for about 10 minutes. Process to form a smooth sauce; set aside and keep warm.

2 Heat half the oil in a wide pan over a high heat. Add the prawns (shrimp) and stir-fry for 2 minutes until pink. Transfer to a plate. Add the squid and stir-fry for about 2 minutes until just firm. Add to the prawns (shrimp).

3 Heat the remaining oil in the pan, add the green (bell) peppers and onion and stir-fry for about 6 minutes until just tender. Stir in the garlic, bay leaves, saffron and chillies and cook for 30 seconds. Add the rice and cook, stirring, until well coated.

4 Add the wine and stir until absorbed. Add the stock, salt and pepper. Bring to the boil and cover. Simmer gently for about 20 minutes until the rice is just tender and the liquid is almost absorbed.

5 Add the clams and mussels. Re-cover and cook for about 10 minutes until the shells open. Stir in the prawns (shrimp) and squid. Re-cover and heat through. Sprinkle with parsley; serve with the sauce.

Vietnamese Rice Paper Wraps

A great idea for a party – just lay out the fillings,
with the two dipping sauces, and let guests assemble their own 'wraps'.

Makes 20–30 wraps

INGREDIENTS

225 g/8 oz cooked peeled prawns

225 g/8 oz salmon fillet, seared for
   1 minute each side and cut into
   5 mm/¼ inch slices

225 g/8 oz tuna steak, seared for
   1 minute each side and cut into
   5 mm/¼ inch slices

2 ripe avocados, peeled, sliced and
   sprinkled with lime juice

6–8 asparagus tips, blanched

1 small red onion, thinly sliced

16 spring onions (scallions), sliced

12 black Niçoise olives, sliced

14 cherry tomatoes, halved

large bunch of coriander (cilantro),
   leaves stripped from the stems

20–30 rice paper wrappers, preferably
   18 cm/7 inch rounds

lime wedges

SPICED VINEGAR DIPPING SAUCE:

80 ml/3 fl oz/⅓ cup rice vinegar

2 tbsp Thai fish sauce

2 tbsp caster (superfine) sugar

1 garlic clove, finely chopped

2 red chillies, deseeded and thinly sliced

2 tbsp chopped fresh coriander (cilantro)

SOY DIPPING SAUCE:

120 ml/4 fl oz/½ cup Thai fish sauce

4–6 tbsp lime juice

2 tbsp Japanese soy sauce

2–3 tbsp light brown sugar

2.5 cm/1 inch piece fresh ginger root,
   finely chopped

2–4 garlic cloves, minced

1 To make the dipping sauces, put the ingredients for each into separate bowls and stir together to blend.

2 Arrange the prawns (shrimp), fish, vegetables and coriander (cilantro) leaves on a large serving platter in groups, ready to use as different fillings for the wrappers. Cover loosely with cling film (plastic wrap) and chill until ready to serve.

3 Dip each wrapper very briefly into a bowl of warm water to soften. Lay on clean tea towels (dish cloths) to absorb any excess water, then pile on to a serving plate and cover with a damp tea towel (dish cloth).

4 To serve, allow each guest to fill their own wrappers. Offer lime wedges for squeezing over the fillings and pass the dipping sauces separately.

Fried Rice Parcels

This is a good way of using leftover rice to make an elegant starter or an unusual light lunch.
Vary the flavours and vegetables or add other leftovers, finely chopped.

Serves 4

INGREDIENTS

8 large sheets of rice paper, cut into
    23 cm/9 inch rounds
1 egg white, lightly whisked
sesame seeds, for sprinkling
Soy Dipping Sauce (see page 72),
    to serve

FRIED RICE:
vegetable oil
1 tsp cumin seeds
225 g/8 oz/ about 2 cups cooked
    white long-grain or basmati rice
1 tbsp rice vinegar
1 tbsp soy sauce
1 tsp chilli sauce, or to taste

2 spring onions (scallions), finely
    chopped
115 g/4 oz frozen peas, defrosted
2 tbsp chopped fresh coriander
    (cilantro)
80 g/3 oz cooked ham or prawns
    (shrimp), diced
salt and pepper

1 Heat 1–2 tablespoons of the oil in a large heavy-based frying pan (skillet). Add the cumin seeds and cook, stirring frequently, for about 1 minute until they begin to pop. Add the rice and stir-fry for 2–3 minutes.

2 Add the vinegar, soy sauce and chilli sauce, and toss with the rice. Add the spring onions (scallions), peas, coriander (cilantro) and ham and stir-fry for

2 minutes to heat through. Season with salt and pepper. Remove from the heat and cool slightly.

3 Fill a shallow pan with warm water and quickly draw each sheet of the rice paper through the water to wet lightly. Drain on tea towels (dish cloths).

4 Arrange the rice paper rounds on a work surface and divide the mixture evenly among them.

Gather up the edges of the paper and twist to form parcels; tie each loosely with string. Transfer to a lightly oiled baking (cookie) sheet.

5 Brush the top and sides lightly with the egg white and sprinkle generously with sesame seeds. Bake in a preheated oven at 200°C/400°F/ Gas Mark 6 for 15–20 minutes until the rice paper is golden. Serve the parcels hot, with the dipping sauce.

Mexican Tomato Rice with Peas

The tomatoes in this recipe give the rice its distinctive pinkish colour.
The texture of the rice will be slightly 'wet'.

Serves 6–8

INGREDIENTS

400 g/14 oz/2 cups long-grain white rice
1 large onion, chopped
2–3 garlic cloves, peeled and smashed
350 g/12 oz/1½ cups canned Italian
   plum tomatoes
3–4 tbsp olive oil
1 litre/1¾ pints/4 cups chicken stock

1 tbsp tomato purée (paste)
1 Habenero or hot chilli
175 g/6 oz frozen green peas,
   defrosted
4 tbsp chopped fresh coriander
   (cilantro)
salt and pepper

TO SERVE:
1 large avocado, peeled, sliced and
   sprinkled with lime juice
lime wedges
4 spring onions (scallions), chopped
1 tbsp chopped fresh coriander
   (cilantro)

1 Cover the rice with hot water and leave to stand for 15 minutes. Drain, then rinse under cold running water.

2 Place the onion and garlic in a food processor and process until a smooth purée forms. Scrape into a small bowl and set aside. Put the tomatoes in the food processor and process until smooth, then strain into another bowl, pushing through any solids with a wooden spoon.

3 Heat the oil in a flameproof casserole over a medium heat. Add the rice and cook for 4 minutes, stirring frequently, until golden and translucent. Add the onion purée and cook, stirring frequently, for a further 2 minutes. Add the stock and tomato purée (paste) and bring to the boil.

4 Using a pin or long needle, carefully pierce the chilli in 2–3 places. Add to the rice, season with salt and pepper and reduce the heat to low. Simmer, covered, for about 25 minutes until the rice is tender and the liquid just absorbed. Discard the chilli, stir in the peas and coriander (cilantro) and cook for 5 minutes to heat through.

5 To serve, gently fork into a large shallow serving bowl. Arrange the avocado slices and lime wedges on top. Sprinkle the chopped spring onions (scallions) and coriander (cilantro) over and serve at once.

Fidellos Tostados

The Sephardic Jews from Spain have been eating a very thin vermicelli-like pasta called fidellos for centuries. Cooked with rice, it is also popular in Greece.

Serves 6

INGREDIENTS

350 g/12 oz vermicelli or angel hair
pasta in coils, roughly broken
100 g/3½ oz/½ cup long-grain
white rice
3 tbsp extra-virgin olive oil

200 g/7 oz/¾ cup canned chopped
tomatoes, drained
600 ml/1 pint/2½ cups chicken stock
or water, plus extra if necessary
1 bay leaf

1–2 tsp chopped fresh oregano or
1 tsp dried oregano
½ tsp dried thyme leaves
salt and pepper
1–2 tbsp sprigs and chopped fresh
oregano or thyme, to garnish

1 Put the pasta and rice in a dry, large, heavy-based saucepan or flameproof casserole over a medium-high heat and cook for 5–7 minutes, stirring frequently, until light golden. (The pasta will break unevenly, but this does not matter.)

2 Stir in 2 tablespoons of the olive oil, together with the chopped tomatoes, stock, bay leaf, oregano and thyme, then season with about a teaspoon of salt and pepper to taste.

3 Bring to the boil, reduce the heat to medium and simmer for about 8 minutes, stirring frequently, to help unwind and separate the pasta coils.

4 Reduce the heat to low and cook, covered, for about 10 minutes until the rice and pasta are tender and all the liquid absorbed. If the rice and pasta are too firm, add about 120 ml/4 fl oz/½ cup more stock or water and continue to cook, covered, for a further 5 minutes. Remove from the heat.

5 Using a fork, fluff the rice and pasta into a warmed deep serving bowl and drizzle with the remaining oil. Sprinkle with the herbs and serve immediately.

Red Rice Pilaf with Roasted Root Vegetables

Red rice from the Camargue region in the South of France has an aromatic,
nutty flavour which complements the robust flavours of the roasted vegetables.

Serves 4–6

INGREDIENTS

120 ml/4 fl oz/^{1}/$_2$ cup olive oil
grated rind and juice of 1 orange
2 tbsp balsamic vinegar
2 tsp coriander seeds, lightly crushed
1 bay leaf
^{1}/$_2$ tsp crushed dried chillies, or to taste
8–10 small raw beetroots, trimmed,
  scrubbed and halved
250 g/9 oz shallots or baby onions
6–8 baby parsnips, trimmed

4–6 baby carrots, trimmed
1 tsp chopped fresh rosemary leaves
400 g/14 oz/2 cups red Camargue rice
850 ml/1^1/$_2$ pints/3^3/$_4$ cups hot chicken
  stock
1 red onion
1 small carrot, cut into matchstick strips
1 leek, cut into 1 cm/^{1}/$_2$ inch rounds
80 g/3 oz/^{1}/$_2$ cup pine kernels (nuts),
  lightly roasted

1 tsp light brown sugar
150 g/5^1/$_2$ oz/about 1 cup dried
  cranberries, sour cherries or raisins,
  soaked in boiling water for 15 minutes
1–2 tbsp chopped fresh coriander (cilantro)
salt and pepper

TO SERVE:
225 ml/8 fl oz/1 cup soured cream
2 tbsp chopped roasted walnuts

1 Put about 4 tablespoons of the olive oil in a large bowl and whisk in the orange rind and juice, vinegar, coriander seeds, bay leaf and crushed chillies. Add the beetroots, shallots, parsnips and carrots and stir to coat well.

2 Turn into a roasting tin (pan) and roast in a preheated oven at 200°C/400°F/Gas Mark 6 for

45–55 minutes until the vegetables are tender, turning occasionally. Remove from the oven, sprinkle with the rosemary and salt and pepper; keep warm.

3 Put the rice in a large saucepan with the hot stock. Place over a medium-high heat and bring to the boil; reduce the heat to low and simmer, covered, for about 40

minutes until the rice is tender and the stock absorbed. Remove from the heat but do not uncover.

4 Heat the remaining oil in a large pan. Add the onion and carrot strips and cook for 8–10 minutes until tender. Add the leek, pine kernels (nuts), brown sugar, and coriander (cilantro) and cook for 2–3 minutes until the vegetables are lightly caramelized. Drain the cranberries and stir into the vegetable mixture with the rice. Season with salt and pepper.

5 Arrange the roasted vegetables and rice on a serving platter and top with the soured cream. Sprinkle with the chopped walnuts and serve.

Curried Rice Patties with Tahini Dressing

*Substantial and flavourful, these patties are a delicious alternative to beef burgers.
Leave the rice with a little bite to give extra texture.*

Serves 4–6

INGREDIENTS

$^1\!/_2$ tsp salt

65 g/2$^1\!/_2$ oz/$^1\!/_3$ cup basmati white or
  brown rice

2 tbsp olive oil

1 red onion, finely chopped

2 garlic cloves

2 tsp curry powder

$^1\!/_2$ tsp crushed dried chilli flakes

1 small red (bell) pepper, cored,
  deseeded and diced

115 g/4 oz frozen peas, defrosted

1 small leek, finely chopped

1 ripe tomato, skinned, deseeded and
  chopped

310 g/11 oz can chick-peas (garbanzo
  beans), drained and rinsed

80 g/3 oz/1$^1\!/_2$ cups fresh white
  breadcrumbs

1–2 tbsp chopped fresh coriander
  (cilantro) or mint

1 egg, lightly beaten

vegetable oil, for frying

salt and pepper

cucumber slices, to garnish

lime wedges, to serve

DRESSING:

120 ml/4 fl oz/$^1\!/_2$ cup tahini

2 garlic cloves, gently crushed

$^1\!/_2$ tsp ground cumin, or to taste

pinch of cayenne pepper

5 tbsp lemon juice

drizzle of extra-virgin olive oil

about 120 ml/4 fl oz/$^1\!/_2$ cup water

1 To make the dressing, blend the tahini, garlic, cumin, cayenne and lemon juice in a food processor until creamy. Slowly pour in the oil, then gradually add water to make a creamy dressing.

2 Bring a saucepan of water to the boil. Add the salt and sprinkle in the rice; simmer for 15–20 minutes until the rice is just tender. Drain, rinse and set aside.

3 Heat the olive oil in a large pan. Add the onion and garlic and cook until beginning to soften. Stir in the curry powder and chilli and cook for 2 minutes. Add the (bell) pepper, peas, leek and tomato and cook gently for 7 minutes until tender. Set aside.

4 Process the chick peas (garbanzo beans) in the food processor until smooth. Add half the vegetables and process again. Transfer to a large bowl and add the remaining vegetable mixture, breadcrumbs, coriander (cilantro) and egg; mix well. Stir in the rice and season well. Chill for 1 hour, then shape into 4–6 patties.

5 Fry the patties in oil for 6–8 minutes until golden. Garnish with cucumber slices and serve with the dressing and lime wedges.

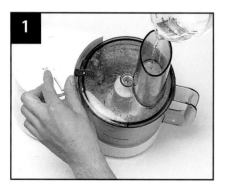

Spicy Potato-rice Pilaf

This spicy blend of potatoes, rice and peas is rich enough to serve on its own or it can be served as part of an Indian meal. If you like it very spicy, serve with a cooling cucumber raita or yogurt.

Serves 4–6

INGREDIENTS

200 g/7 oz/1 cup basmati rice, soaked
  in cold water for 20 minutes
2 tbsp vegetable oil
$^1/_2$–$^3/_4$ tsp cumin seeds
225 g/8 oz potatoes, cut into 1 cm/
  $^1/_2$ inch pieces
225 g/8 oz frozen peas, defrosted

1 green chilli, deseeded and thinly
  sliced (optional)
$^1/_2$ tsp salt
1 tsp garam masala
$^1/_2$ tsp ground turmeric
$^1/_4$ tsp cayenne pepper
600 ml/1 pint/$2^1/_2$ cups water

2 tbsp chopped fresh coriander
  (cilantro)
1 red onion, finely chopped
natural yogurt, to serve

1 Rinse the soaked rice under cold running water until the water runs clear, drain and set aside.

2 Heat the oil in a large heavy-based saucepan over a medium-high heat. Add the cumin seeds and stir for about 10 seconds until the seeds jump and colour.

3 Add the potatoes, peas and chilli, if using, and stir-fry for about 3 minutes until the potatoes are just beginning to soften.

4 Add the rice and cook, stirring frequently, until well coated and beginning to turn translucent. Stir in the salt, garam masala, turmeric and cayenne pepper, then add the water. Bring to the boil, stirring once or twice, then reduce the heat to medium and simmer, covered, until most of the water is absorbed and the surface is filled with little steam-holes. Do not stir.

5 Reduce the heat to very low and, if possible, raise the pan about 2.5 cm/1 inch above the heat source by resting on a ring. Cover and steam for about 10 minutes longer. Remove from the heat, uncover and put a clean tea towel (dish cloth) or paper towels over the rice; re-cover. Stand for 5 minutes.

6 Gently fork the rice and potato mixture into a warmed serving bowl and sprinkle with the coriander (cilantro) and chopped red onion. Serve hot with yogurt handed separately.

Turkish Carrot Pilaf

Because of their bright golden colour, carrots symbolize hope and prosperity in many cultures. They sweeten the rice in this delicious Turkish pilaf and add a slightly crunchy texture.

Serves 6

INGREDIENTS

60 g/2 oz/4 tbsp butter
2 carrots, coarsely grated
1/2 tsp whole black peppercorns
pinch of salt

4–6 ready-soaked dried apricots,
  thinly sliced (optional)
1 tsp sugar
400 g/14 oz/2 cups long-grain white
  rice

700 ml/1 1/4 pints/3 cups chicken stock
1–2 tbsp chopped green pistachios,
  for sprinkling (optional)

1 Melt the butter in a large, heavy-based saucepan over a medium heat. Add the grated carrots and whole peppercorns with a pinch of salt and cook, stirring frequently, for about 3 minutes until the carrots begin to soften.

2 Add the apricots, if using, and sprinkle with the sugar, stirring to combine. Stir in the rice and cook, stirring frequently, for about 3 minutes until the rice is coated with butter and is translucent.

3 Pour in the stock and bring to the boil. Reduce the heat to low and simmer, covered, for 20–25 minutes until the rice is tender and the stock is completely absorbed. Remove from the heat and uncover. Place a folded tea towel (dish cloth) or paper towels over the rice and re-cover. Stand for about 10 minutes for any steam to be absorbed.

4 Fork the rice into a shallow serving bowl and shape into a rounded dome; sprinkle with the pistachios, if using, and serve hot.

COOK'S TIP

As an alternative serving idea, spoon the pilaf into an oiled ring mould, pressing lightly to compress the rice. Cover the mould with an up-turned serving plate and, holding the plate and mould firmly together, invert quickly, giving a good shake. Gently remove the mould. Fill the centre with chopped pistachios and garnish with a sprig of parsley and cooked carrot strips.

Coconut-scented Brown Rice

In this basic recipe, brown rice is cooked slowly by the absorption method, producing a tender, creamy rice with lots of flavour. An excellent accompaniment to grilled (broiled) chicken, pork or even fish.

Serves 4–6

INGREDIENTS

350 ml/12 fl oz/1½ cups water
225 ml/8 fl oz/1 cup coconut milk
1 tsp salt

200 g/7 oz/1 cup long-grain brown rice
1 lemon
1 cinnamon stick

about 15 whole cloves
1 tbsp chopped fresh parsley
fresh coconut shavings (optional)

1 Bring the water to the boil in a heavy-based saucepan and whisk in the coconut milk. Return the liquid to the boil, add the salt and sprinkle in the rice.

2 Pare 2–3 strips of lemon rind and add to the saucepan with the cinnamon stick and the cloves.

3 Reduce the heat to low, cover, and simmer gently for about 45 minutes until the rice is tender and the liquid is completely absorbed. Uncover and leave the rice over high heat for about 1 minute, to allow any steam to escape and the rice to dry out a little bit.

4 Remove the cloves, if wished, then sprinkle with the herbs and coconut, if using; fork into a warmed serving bowl and serve.

VARIATION

The whole cloves can be replaced with a pinch of ground allspice.

COOK'S TIP

This technique can be used to cook white rice as well, but the fuller flavour of brown rice works well with the warm flavour of the spices.

VARIATION

For a more South-East Asian flavour, use 1 red chilli, pierced in 2–3 places with a pin, a bruised lime leaf and a 7.5 cm/3 inch piece of lemon grass, lightly crushed, instead of the lemon and cloves.

Fragrant Orange Basmati Rice

This delicious rice, scented with star anise for a slightly exotic effect, is excellent served with Mediterranean and Middle Eastern meat stews.

Serves 4–6

INGREDIENTS

1–2 tbsp butter
3–4 shallots, finely chopped
200 g/7 oz/1 cup basmati rice
2.5 cm/1 inch piece of fresh ginger
   root, peeled

1–2 fresh bay leaves, lightly bruised
2 star anise
1 small cinnamon stick
grated rind and juice of 1 orange
1 tbsp raisins, finely chopped

300 ml/10 fl oz/1¼ cups light chicken
   stock or water
salt and pepper
fresh coriander (cilantro) leaves, to
   garnish (optional)

1 Melt the butter in a heavy-based saucepan placed over a medium heat. Add the shallots and cook for 2–3 minutes until beginning to soften.

2 Add the rice and cook, stirring frequently, for 3 minutes until the rice is well coated with the butter and is translucent. Using a large heavy knife, crush the piece of ginger lightly. Add to the pan with the bay leaves, star anise and cinnamon stick. Add the grated rind and orange juice and the raisins and stir.

3 Add the stock and bring to the boil. Season with salt and pepper and reduce the heat. Cover and cook over a low heat for 15–18 minutes until the rice is tender and the liquid completely absorbed. Remove from the heat, uncover and place a clean tea towel (dish cloth) over the rice. Re-cover and stand for up to 20 minutes.

4 Fork the rice into a serving bowl and remove the bay leaves, star anise and cinnamon stick (or keep them in for decoration). Sprinkle the top with a few coriander (cilantro) leaves, if wished, and serve hot.

COOK'S TIP

Most packaged brands of basmati do not need washing and soaking. However, it does not hurt to wash the rice, it simply removes any starch. Cover the rice with water and soak for about 20 minutes, stirring occasionally. Drain, then rinse under cold running water until the water runs clear. Drain and proceed with the recipe.

Lemon-scented Rice with Mint

The fresh clean flavours of this pilaf make it an ideal accompaniment for a wide variety of dishes from plain roasted meats to exotic curries and stews.

Serves 6–8

INGREDIENTS

2 tbsp olive oil or butter
2–4 spring onions (scallions), finely chopped
3–4 tbsp chopped fresh mint

300 g/10$\frac{1}{2}$ oz/l$\frac{1}{2}$ cups long-grain white rice
500 ml/18 fl oz/2$\frac{1}{4}$ cups chicken stock, preferably homemade
1 lemon

salt and pepper

TO GARNISH:
2–3 mint sprigs
thin lemon and lime slices

1 Heat the oil or butter in a medium heavy-based saucepan over a medium-high heat. Add the spring onions (scallions) and mint and cook, stirring, for about 1 minute until brightly coloured and fragrant.

2 Add the rice and cook, stirring frequently, for about 2 minutes until well coated with the oil or butter and just translucent. Add the chicken stock and bring to the boil, stirring once or twice. Season with salt and pepper to taste.

3 Pare 3–4 strips of lemon rind and add to the pan; squeeze the juice from the lemon and stir into the rice and stock.

4 When the stock comes to the boil, reduce the heat to low and simmer gently, tightly covered, for about 20 minutes until the rice is tender and the stock absorbed. Remove the pan from the heat and stand for 5–10 minutes.

5 Fork the rice into a serving bowl, garnish with mint and lemon and lime slices. Serve hot.

COOK'S TIP

This basic technique for pilaf rice can be used with other flavour combinations and herbs. The important thing is to fry the rice until well coated and add just enough water to be absorbed by the rice.

Fruity Rice Stuffing

This rich fruit-filled stuffing, inspired by a Turkish pilaf, is a wonderful way to use leftover rice.
Here it is used with poussins, but it is also delicious with lamb, goose, duck and game birds.

Serves 4

INGREDIENTS

4 fresh poussins
4–6 tbsp butter, melted

STUFFING:
225 ml/8 fl oz/1 cup port
125 g/4¹/₂ oz/1 cup raisins
115 g/4 oz/1 cup dried no-soak
 apricots, sliced
2–3 tbsp extra-virgin olive oil

1 onion, finely chopped
1 stalk celery, thinly sliced
2 garlic cloves, finely chopped
1 tsp ground cinnamon
1 tsp dried oregano
1 tsp dried mint or basil
¹/₂ tsp allspice or ¹/₄ tsp cloves
225 g/8 oz unsweetened chestnuts,
 canned or vacuum-packed

200 g/7 oz/1 cup long-grain white
 rice, cooked
grated rind and juice of 2 oranges
350 ml/12 fl oz/1¹/₂ cups chicken stock
50 g/l³/₄ oz/¹/₂ cup walnut halves,
 lightly toasted and chopped
2 tbsp chopped fresh mint
2 tbsp chopped fresh flat-leaf parsley
salt and pepper

1 To make the stuffing, combine the port, raisins and apricots in a small bowl and leave to stand for about 15 minutes.

2 Heat the oil in a large heavy-based saucepan. Add the onion and celery and cook for 3–4 minutes. Add the garlic, all the spices and the chestnuts and cook for about 4 minutes, stirring occasionally. Add the rice and half the orange rind and juice, then pour in the stock. Simmer gently for 5 minutes until most of the liquid is absorbed.

3 Drain the raisins and apricots, reserving the port, and stir into the rice mixture with the walnuts, mint and parsley; cook for a further 2 minutes. Season with salt and pepper, then remove from the heat and cool.

4 Rub the poussins inside and out with salt and pepper. Lightly fill the cavity of each bird with the stuffing; do not pack too tightly. Tie the legs of each bird together, tucking in the tail. Form extra stuffing into balls.

5 Arrange the birds in a roasting tin (pan) with any stuffing balls and brush with melted butter. Drizzle any remaining butter around the pan. Pour over the remaining orange rind and juice and the reserved port.

6 Roast in a preheated oven at 180°C/350°F/Gas Mark 4 for about 45 minutes, basting, until cooked. Transfer to a platter, cover with foil and rest for 5 minutes. Serve with any pan juices.

Mixed Rice Stuffing with Wild Mushrooms

Prepared by the pilaf method to infuse both rices with as much flavour as possible, this stuffing is also excellent as a side dish.

Makes enough to stuff 1 large chicken or small turkey

INGREDIENTS

60 g/2 oz/4 tbsp butter or oil
6 shallots, finely chopped
175 g/6 oz/1 cup wild rice
600 ml/1 pint/2½ cups chicken stock
1 bay leaf
½ tsp dried thyme or 2–3 sprigs fresh

200 g/7 oz/1 cup long-grain white rice
60 g/2 oz dried wild mushrooms
225 g/8 oz fresh mushrooms, sliced
2 garlic cloves, finely chopped
3–4 tbsp Madeira wine

80 g/3 oz/½ cup pecan or walnut
halves, toasted and coarsely chopped
3–4 tbsp chopped fresh flat-leaf
parsley
2 tbsp chopped fresh chives
salt and pepper

1 Heat half the butter or oil in a large saucepan. Add half the shallots and cook until beginning to soften. Stir in the wild rice to coat, then add 350 ml/12 fl oz/1½ cups of the chicken stock, the bay leaf and thyme and bring to the boil. Simmer gently, covered, for about 20 minutes until the stock is absorbed. The wild rice will not be completely cooked.

2 Add the white rice and the remaining stock and season with salt and pepper. Bring to the boil again, stirring once or twice, then simmer gently, covered, for 20–25 minutes until the stock is absorbed and all the rice is tender. Remove from the heat and stand, covered, for 10–15 minutes.

3 Meanwhile, cover the wild mushrooms with boiling water and leave to soften for about 30 minutes. Lift the mushrooms out and pat dry. Slice thinly.

4 Heat the remaining butter or oil in a large frying pan (skillet). Add the remaining shallots and cook for 3 minutes. Add the fresh mushrooms, garlic and Madeira and stir-fry for 3–4 minutes until golden. Stir in the wild mushrooms and cook, stirring occasionally, until all the liquid is absorbed. Turn into a large bowl.

5 Using a fork, fluff the rice into the bowl with the mushrooms, add the chopped nuts, parsley and chives and adjust the seasoning; toss together. Cool before using as a stuffing.

Risottos

One of the great gastronomic feats of Italian cooking, risotto is made with a special rice to create a deliciously creamy dish. It is surprisingly simple to make, but does require a little patience because it involves slow cooking and constant stirring. As long as you use the correct rice and a good homemade stock, and take your time, you'll be on your way to making a perfect risotto!

The recipes in this chapter illustrate the versatility of risotto. Here you'll find something for every occasion – Easy Cheesy Risotto with Parmesan shows you the basic, easy-to-make method, risotto with asparagus or wild mushrooms is guaranteed to give a mid-week meal a lift, while glamorous Champagne Risotto and interesting Black Risotto or Fennel Risotto with Vodka make memorable dinner party dishes. Risotto flavoured with sun-dried tomatoes and Italian cheese, or Minted Risotto with Herbs makes perfect food for family gatherings.

As a change from the classic risotto, try scrumptious Cheese-topped Risotto Tart with Spinach or little Arrancini, irresistible fried risotto balls. There's even a tasty oven-baked risotto, with pancetta and mushrooms.

Easy Cheesy Risotto with Parmesan

Although this is the easiest, most basic risotto, it is one of the most delicious.
Because there are few ingredients, use the best of each.

Serves 4–6

INGREDIENTS

60–75 g/2–2¾ oz/4–5 tbsp unsalted
  butter
1 onion, finely chopped
300 g/10½ oz/1½ cups arborio or
  carnaroli rice

120 ml/4 fl oz/½ cup dry white
  vermouth or white wine
1.2 litres/2 pints/5 cups chicken or
  vegetable stock, simmering

80 g/3 oz/1 cup freshly grated
  Parmesan cheese, plus extra for
  sprinkling
salt and pepper

1 Heat about 25 g/1 oz/2 tbsp of the butter in a large heavy-based saucepan over a medium heat. Add the onion and cook for about 2 minutes until just beginning to soften. Add the rice and cook for about 2 minutes, stirring frequently, until translucent and well coated with the butter.

2 Pour in the vermouth: it will bubble and steam rapidly and evaporate almost immediately. Add a ladleful (about 225 ml/8 fl oz/1 cup) of the simmering stock and cook, stirring constantly, until the stock is absorbed.

3 Continue adding the stock, about half a ladleful at a time, allowing each addition to be absorbed before adding the next – never allow the rice to cook 'dry'. This should take 20–25 minutes. The risotto should have a creamy consistency and the rice grains should be tender, but still firm to the bite.

4 Remove the pan from the heat and stir in the remaining butter and Parmesan. Season with salt and a little pepper, to taste. Cover, stand for about 1 minute, then serve immediately with extra Parmesan for sprinkling.

COOK'S TIP

If you prefer not to use butter, soften
the onion in 2 tablespoons olive oil
and stir in about 2 tablespoons
extra-virgin olive oil with the
Parmesan at the end.

Risotto with Asparagus

An Italian classic, this simple recipe makes a stylish lunch or supper dish.
It's worth using the best asparagus you can find.

Serves 6

INGREDIENTS

900 g/2 lb fresh asparagus, washed
2 tbsp sunflower or other vegetable oil
80 g/3 oz/6 tbsp unsalted butter
2 shallots or 1 small onion, finely
  chopped

400 g/14 oz/2 cups arborio or
  carnaroli rice
1.5 litres/2¾ pints/6¼ cups light chicken
  or vegetable stock, simmering

80 g/3 oz/1 cup freshly grated
  Parmesan cheese
salt and pepper
Parmesan shavings, to garnish (optional)

1 Lightly peel the stems of the asparagus; trim off the woody ends. Cut the tips off each stalk and set aside. Cut the remaining stems into 2.5 cm/1 inch pieces.

2 Add the asparagus stem pieces to a pan of boiling water and boil for 2 minutes. Add the asparagus tips and boil for about 1 minute until tender-crisp; do not overcook. Rinse under cold running water and set aside.

3 Heat the oil with half the butter in a large heavy-based saucepan. Add the shallots and cook gently for about 2 minutes until softened. Add the rice and cook, stirring frequently, for about 2 minutes until the rice is translucent and well coated.

4 Add a ladleful (about 225 ml/8 fl oz/1 cup) of the simmering stock; it will bubble and steam rapidly. Cook, stirring constantly, until the stock is completely absorbed.

5 Continue adding the stock, about half a ladleful at a time, allowing each addition to be absorbed before adding the next – never allow the rice to cook 'dry'. This should take 20–25 minutes. The risotto should have a creamy consistency and the rice should be tender, but firm to the bite.

6 Heat the asparagus tips in the stock. Stir the stems into the risotto with the last ladleful of stock, the remaining butter and Parmesan. Remove from the heat and stir in the asparagus tips and season if necessary. Serve with Parmesan shavings, if wished.

Lemon Risotto with Peas & Mint

Fresh peas and mint are added to this light and lemony risotto, which is excellent served as a first course for a summer meal.

Serves 4–6

INGREDIENTS

1.5 litres/2³/₄ pints/6¹/₄ cups chicken stock
4–5 fresh mint sprigs
2 tbsp extra-virgin olive oil
80 g/3 oz/6 tbsp unsalted butter
2–3 large shallots, finely chopped

300 g/10¹/₂ oz/1¹/₂ cups arborio or carnaroli rice
grated rind and juice of 1 large unwaxed lemon
175 g/6 oz fresh shelled peas, lightly cooked

60 g/2 oz/²/₃ cup freshly grated Parmesan cheese
salt and pepper
lemon wedges, to garnish

1 Bring the stock to the boil in a large saucepan. Strip the leaves from the mint sprigs and set aside; gently 'bruise' the mint stems and add to the stock. Reduce the heat and keep the stock at a gentle simmer.

2 Heat the oil and half the butter in a large heavy-based saucepan over medium heat. Add the shallots and cook for about 2 minutes until soft. Add the rice and cook, stirring frequently, for about 2 minutes until the rice is translucent and well coated.

3 Leaving aside the mint stems, add a ladleful (about 225 ml/8 fl oz/1 cup) of the simmering stock; it will steam and bubble rapidly. Cook, stirring constantly until the stock is absorbed.

4 Continue adding the stock, about half a ladleful at a time, allowing each addition to be absorbed before adding the next. This should take 20–25 minutes. The risotto should have a creamy consistency and the rice should be tender but firm to the bite.

5 Stir in the lemon rind and juice and the peas; cook until heated through, adding a little more stock or water if the risotto becomes too thick. Remove the pan from the heat and stir in the Parmesan and remaining butter. Season to taste with salt and pepper.

6 Chop the reserved mint leaves and stir into the risotto. Serve immediately with lemon wedges.

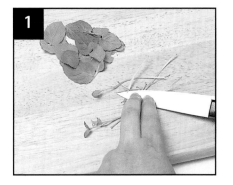

Minted Green Risotto with Herbs

This tasty risotto gets its vibrant green colour from the spinach and mint. Serve with Italian-style rustic bread and salad for an informal supper.

Serves 6

INGREDIENTS

25 g/1 oz/2 tbsp unsalted butter

450 g/1 lb fresh shelled peas, or defrosted frozen peas

1 kg/2 lb 4 oz fresh young spinach leaves, washed and drained

1 bunch fresh mint, leaves stripped from stalks

2 tbsp chopped fresh basil

2 tbsp chopped fresh oregano

large pinch of freshly grated nutmeg

4 tbsp mascarpone or double (heavy) cream

2 tbsp vegetable oil

1 onion, finely chopped

4 stalks celery, including leaves, finely chopped

2 garlic cloves, finely chopped

$\frac{1}{2}$ tsp dried thyme

300 g/10$\frac{1}{2}$ oz/1$\frac{1}{2}$ cups arborio or carnaroli rice

50 ml/2 fl oz/$\frac{1}{4}$ cup dry white vermouth

1 litre/1$\frac{3}{4}$ pints/4 cups light chicken or vegetable stock, simmering

80 g/3 oz/1 cup freshly grated Parmesan cheese

1 Heat half the butter in a deep frying pan (skillet) over a medium-high heat until sizzling. Add the peas, spinach, mint leaves, basil and oregano; season with the nutmeg. Cook for about 3 minutes, stirring frequently, until the spinach and mint leaves are wilted. Cool slightly.

2 Pour the spinach mixture into a food processor and process for 15 seconds. Add the mascarpone and process again for about 1 minute. Transfer to a bowl and set aside.

3 Heat the oil and remaining butter in a large, heavy-based saucepan over a medium heat. Add the onion, celery, garlic and thyme and cook for about 2 minutes until the vegetables are softened. Add the rice and cook, stirring frequently, for about 2 minutes until the rice is translucent and well coated.

4 Add the vermouth to the rice; it will bubble and steam rapidly. When it is almost absorbed, add a ladleful (about 225 ml/8 fl oz/ 1 cup) of the simmering stock. Cook, stirring constantly, until the stock is completely absorbed.

5 Continue adding the stock, about half a ladleful at a time, allowing each addition to be absorbed before adding the next. This should take 20–25 minutes. The risotto should have a creamy consistency and the rice should be just tender. Stir in the spinach-cream mixture and the Parmesan. Serve immediately.

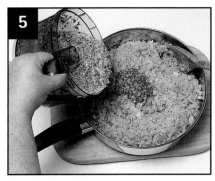

Fennel Risotto with Vodka

The alcohol in the vodka cooks out but leaves a pleasant, tantalizing flavour which complements the cool sweetness of the fennel.

Serves 4–6

INGREDIENTS

2 large fennel bulbs
2 tbsp vegetable oil
80 g/3 oz/6 tbsp unsalted butter
1 large onion, finely chopped
350 g/12 oz/1¾ cups arborio or
    carnaroli rice

150 ml/5 fl oz/⅔ cup vodka (or lemon-
    flavoured vodka, if you can find it)
1.3 litres/2¼ pints/5⅔ cups light
    chicken or vegetable stock, simmering
60 g/2 oz/⅔ cup freshly grated
    Parmesan cheese

5–6 tbsp lemon juice
salt and pepper

1 Trim the fennel, reserving the fronds for the garnish, if wished. Cut the bulbs in half lengthways and remove the V-shaped cores; coarsely chop the flesh. (If you like, add any of the fennel trimmings to the stock for extra flavour.)

2 Heat the oil and half the butter in a large heavy-based saucepan over a medium heat. Add the onion and fennel and cook for about 2 minutes, stirring frequently, until the vegetables are softened. Add the rice and cook for about 2 minutes, stirring frequently, until the rice is translucent and well coated.

3 Pour in the vodka; it will bubble rapidly and evaporate almost immediately. Add a ladleful (about 225 ml/8 fl oz/1 cup) of the stock. Cook, stirring constantly, until the stock is absorbed.

4 Continue adding the stock, about half a ladleful at a time, allowing each addition to be absorbed before adding the next – never allow the rice to cook 'dry'.

This should take 20–25 minutes. The risotto should have a creamy consistency and the rice should be tender, but firm to the bite.

5 Stir in the remaining butter, with the Parmesan and lemon juice. Remove from the heat, cover and stand for 1 minute. Serve immediately, garnished with a few of the fennel fronds, if wished.

Risotto with Cannellini Beans

The Italians, particularly the Tuscans, love dishes made with beans.
This recipe combines beans and rice to make a rich, creamy risotto with a great flavour.

Serves 6–8

INGREDIENTS

300 g/10½ oz cannellini or white
   kidney beans, soaked and cooked
   according to packet instructions
2–3 tbsp olive oil
1 large red (or sweet white) onion,
   finely chopped
3–4 stalks celery, finely chopped

115 g/4 oz pancetta or thick-cut
   smoky bacon
2–3 garlic cloves, minced
¾ tsp dried oregano or 1 tbsp
   chopped fresh oregano
400 g/14 oz/2 cups arborio or
   carnaroli rice

1 litre/1¾ pints/4 cups chicken stock,
   simmering
60 g/2 oz/4 tbsp unsalted butter at
   room temperature
115 g/4 oz/1⅓ cups freshly grated
   Parmesan cheese
salt and pepper

1   Mash, or press through a food mill, half of the cannellini beans and set aside.

2   Heat the olive oil in a large heavy-based saucepan over a medium heat. Add the onion and celery and cook for about 2 minutes until softened. Add the pancetta, garlic and oregano and cook for a further 1–2 minutes, stirring occasionally. Add the rice and cook, stirring frequently, for about 2 minutes until it is translucent and well coated with the oil.

3   Add a ladleful (about 225 ml/8 fl oz/1 cup) of the simmering stock; it will bubble and steam rapidly. Cook, stirring constantly, until the stock is absorbed.

4   Continue adding the stock, about half a ladleful at a time, allowing each addition to be absorbed before adding the next. This should take 20–25 minutes.

The risotto should have a creamy consistency and the rice should be tender, but still firm to the bite.

5   Stir in the beans and the bean purée, season with salt and pepper and heat through. Add a little more stock if necessary.

6   Remove from the heat and stir in the butter and half the Parmesan. Cover and stand for about 1 minute. Serve with the remaining Parmesan sprinkled over.

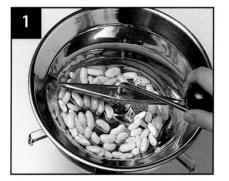

Champagne Risotto

This deluxe dish, with its pronounced Champagne flavour, is one to reserve for special occasions. Serve the rest of the wine with the dish, as the perfect accompaniment!

Serves 4–6

INGREDIENTS

2 tbsp vegetable oil
115 g/4 oz/8 tbsp unsalted butter
2 shallots, finely chopped
300 g/10$\frac{1}{2}$ oz/1$\frac{1}{2}$ cups arborio or carnaroli rice

about 600 ml/1 pint/2$\frac{1}{2}$ cups Champagne or dry sparkling white wine
700 ml/1$\frac{1}{4}$ pints/3 cups light chicken stock, simmering

60 g/2 oz/$\frac{2}{3}$ cup freshly grated Parmesan cheese
salt and pepper
4–6 large cooked prawns (shrimp), to garnish (optional)

1 Heat the oil and half the butter in a large heavy-based saucepan over a medium heat. Add the shallots and cook for about 2 minutes, until softened. Add the rice and cook, stirring frequently, for about 2 minutes until the rice is translucent and well coated (see Cook's Tip).

2 Pour in half the Champagne; it will bubble and steam rapidly. Cook, stirring constantly, until the liquid is absorbed. Add a ladleful (about 225 ml/8 fl oz/1 cup) of the simmering stock to the pan and cook, stirring constantly, until the liquid is absorbed.

3 Continue adding the stock, about half a ladleful at a time, allowing each addition to be absorbed before adding the next – never allow the rice to cook 'dry'. This should take 20–25 minutes. The risotto should have a creamy consistency and the rice should be tender, but firm to the bite.

4 Stir in the remaining champagne and cook for a further 2–3 minutes. Remove from the heat and stir in the remaining butter and Parmesan. Season with salt and pepper to taste.

5 Spoon the risotto into serving bowls and garnish each portion with a prawn (shrimp), if wished. Serve immediately.

COOK'S TIP

It is important to heat and coat the rice at this stage as it will help give the rice its creamy texture.

Wild Mushroom Risotto

*Distinctive-tasting wild mushrooms, so popular in Italy,
give this dish a wonderful, robust flavour.*

Serves 6

INGREDIENTS

60 g/2 oz dried porcini or morel
   mushrooms
about 500 g/1 lb 2 oz mixed fresh wild
   mushrooms, such as porcini, girolles,
   horse mushrooms and chanterelles,
   cleaned and halved if large
4 tbsp olive oil

3–4 garlic cloves, finely chopped
60 g/2 oz/4 tbsp unsalted butter
1 onion, finely chopped
350 g/12 oz/1¾ cups arborio or
   carnaroli rice
50 ml/2 fl oz/¼ cup dry white
   vermouth

1.2 litres/2 pints/5 cups chicken stock,
   simmering
115 g/4 oz/1⅓ cups freshly grated
   Parmesan cheese
4 tbsp chopped fresh flat-leaf parsley
salt and pepper

1 Cover the dried mushrooms with boiling water. Leave to soak for 30 minutes, then carefully lift out and pat dry. Strain the soaking liquid through a sieve (strainer) lined with a paper towel, and set aside.

2 Trim the wild mushrooms and gently brush clean.

3 Heat 3 tablespoons of the oil in a large frying pan (skillet) until hot. Add the fresh

mushrooms, and stir-fry for 1–2 minutes. Add the garlic and the soaked mushrooms and cook for 2 minutes, stirring frequently. Scrape on to a plate and set aside.

4 Heat the remaining oil and half the butter in a large heavy-based saucepan. Add the onion and cook for about 2 minutes until softened. Add the rice and cook, stirring frequently, for about 2 minutes until translucent and well coated.

5 Add the vermouth to the rice. When almost absorbed, add a ladleful (about 225 ml/8 fl oz/1 cup) of the simmering stock. Cook, stirring constantly, until the liquid is absorbed.

6 Continue adding the stock, about half a ladleful at a time, allowing each addition to be absorbed before adding the next. This should take 20–25 minutes. The risotto should have a creamy consistency and the rice should be tender, but firm to the bite.

7 Add half the dried mushroom soaking liquid to the risotto and stir in the mushrooms. Season with salt and pepper, and add more mushroom liquid if necessary. Remove from the heat; stir in the remaining butter, Parmesan and parsley. Serve immediately.

Risotto Primavera

This is a nice way to use those first green vegetables which signal the spring, la primavera.
Feel free to add other favourite vegetables, if you like.

Serves 6–8

INGREDIENTS

225 g/8 oz fresh thin asparagus
  spears, well rinsed
4 tbsp olive oil
175 g/6 oz young green beans, cut
  into 2.5 cm/1 inch pieces
175 g/6 oz young courgettes
  (zucchini), quartered and cut into
  2.5 cm/1 inch lengths

225 g/8 oz fresh shelled peas
1 onion, finely chopped
1–2 garlic cloves, finely chopped
350 g/12 oz/1¾ cups arborio or
  carnaroli rice
1.5 litres/2¾ pints/6¼ cups chicken
  stock, simmering, plus extra 2 tbsp

4 spring onions (scallions), cut into
  2.5 cm/1 inch lengths
60 g/2 oz/4 tbsp unsalted butter
115 g/4 oz/1⅓ cups freshly grated
  Parmesan cheese
2 tbsp chopped fresh chives
2 tbsp fresh shredded basil
salt and pepper

1 Trim the woody ends of the asparagus and cut off the tips. Cut the stems into 2.5 cm/1 inch pieces and set aside with the tips.

2 Heat 2 tablespoons of the olive oil in a large frying pan (skillet) over a high heat, until very hot. Add the asparagus, beans, courgettes (zucchini) and peas and stir-fry for 3–4 minutes until they are bright green and just beginning to soften. Set aside.

3 Heat the remaining olive oil in a large heavy-based saucepan over a medium heat. Add the onion and cook for about 1 minute until it begins to soften. Stir in the garlic and cook for 30 seconds. Add the rice and cook, stirring frequently, for 2 minutes until translucent and coated with oil.

4 Add a ladleful (about 225 ml/ 8 fl oz/1 cup) of the hot stock; the stock will bubble rapidly. Cook, stirring constantly, until the stock is absorbed.

5 Continue adding the stock, about half a ladleful at a time, allowing each addition to be absorbed before adding the next – never allow the rice to cook 'dry'. This should take 20–25 minutes. The risotto should have a creamy consistency and the rice should be tender, but firm to the bite.

6 Stir in the stir-fried vegetables and spring onions (scallions) with a little more stock. Cook for 2 minutes, stirring frequently, then season with salt and pepper. Stir in the butter, Parmesan, chives and basil. Remove from the heat, cover and stand for about 1 minute. Garnish with spring onions, if wished. Serve immediately.

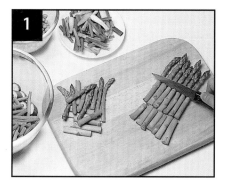

Roasted Pumpkin Risotto

*The combination of sweet creamy pumpkin with
the slight saltiness of dolcelatte and the pungency of sage is delicious.*

Serves 6

INGREDIENTS

4 tbsp olive oil
60 g/2 oz/4 tbsp unsalted butter, cut
  into small pieces
450 g/1 lb pumpkin flesh, cut into 1
  cm/¹/₂ inch dice
³/₄ tsp rubbed sage
2 garlic cloves, finely chopped
2 tbsp lemon juice

2 large shallots, finely chopped
350 g/12 oz/1³/₄ cups arborio or
  carnaroli rice
50 ml/2 fl oz/¹/₄ cup dry white
  vermouth
1.2 litres/2 pints/5 cups chicken stock,
  simmering
vegetable oil, for frying

60 g/2 oz/²/₃ cup freshly grated
  Parmesan cheese
300 g/10¹/₂ oz dolcelatte, cut into
  small pieces
salt and pepper
celery leaves, to garnish

1 Put half the olive oil and about 15 g/½ oz/1 tbsp of the butter in a roasting tin (pan) and heat in a preheated oven at 200°C/400°F/Gas Mark 6.

2 Add the pumpkin to the pan and sprinkle with the sage, half the garlic and salt and pepper. Toss together and roast for about 10 minutes until just softened and beginning to caramelize. Transfer to a plate.

3 Roughly mash about half the cooked pumpkin with the lemon juice and reserve with the remaining diced pumpkin.

4 Heat the remaining oil and 15 g/½ oz/1 tbsp of the butter in a large, heavy-based saucepan over a medium heat. Stir in the shallots and remaining garlic and cook for about 1 minute. Add the rice and cook, stirring, for about 2 minutes until well coated.

5 Pour in the vermouth; it will bubble and steam rapidly. Add a ladleful (about 225 ml/8 fl oz/1 cup) of the simmering stock and cook, stirring constantly, until the stock is absorbed.

6 Continue adding the stock, about half a ladleful at a time, allowing each addition to be absorbed before adding the next – never allow the rice to cook 'dry'. This should take 20–25 minutes. The risotto should have a creamy consistency and the rice should be tender, but firm to the bite.

7 Stir all the pumpkin into the risotto with the remaining butter and the Parmesan. Remove from the heat and fold in the diced dolcelatte. Serve at once, garnished with celery leaves.

Truffle Risotto

If you feel like splashing out on a luxurious dish, this is the one for you! Traditionally this risotto is made with white truffles, but black truffles are used in this version as they are more widely available.

Serves 6

INGREDIENTS

2 leeks
115 g/4 oz/8 tbsp unsalted butter
300 g/10½ oz/1½ cups arborio or
   carnaroli rice
1.2 litres/2 pints/5 cups chicken stock,
   simmering

50 ml/2 fl oz/¼ cup dry white
   vermouth or white wine
120 ml/4 fl oz/½ cup double (heavy)
   cream
freshly grated nutmeg
115 g/4 oz/1⅓ cups freshly grated
   Parmesan cheese

115–175 g/4–6 oz fresh black truffles,
   brushed clean
50–80 ml/2–3 fl oz/¼–⅓ cup truffle
   oil (optional)
salt and ¼–½ tsp ground white
   pepper

1 Slice the leeks in half lengthways, then shred thinly.

2 Heat half the butter in a large heavy-based pan over medium heat. Add the leeks and cook for about 1 minute until just starting to soften. Add the rice and cook, stirring, until translucent and well coated in butter.

3 Add a ladleful (about 225 ml/ 8 fl oz/1 cup) of the hot stock; it will bubble and steam rapidly. Cook, stirring, until the stock is absorbed.

4 Continue adding the stock, about half a ladleful at a time, allowing each addition to be absorbed before adding the next. This should take 20–25 minutes. The risotto should have a creamy consistency and the rice should be tender, but firm to the bite.

5 Just before the rice is cooked, stir in the vermouth and cream. Season with a little nutmeg, salt and white pepper. Continue cooking for 3–4 minutes until the liquid is absorbed. Remove from the heat and stir in the Parmesan and remaining butter.

6 Spoon into serving dishes and shave equal amounts of truffle over each portion. Drizzle over a little truffle oil, if using.

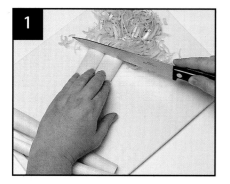

Beetroot, Dried Cherry & Red Wine Risotto

*The beetroot and red wine give this risotto its stunning 'hot pink' colour
and also impart a rich sweet flavour, which is unusual but surprisingly delicious.*

Serves 4–6

INGREDIENTS

175 g/6 oz/1 cup dried sour cherries or
  dried cranberries
225 ml/8 fl oz/1 cup fruity red wine,
  such as Valpolicella
3 tbsp olive oil
1 large red onion, finely chopped
2 stalks celery, finely chopped

$^1/_2$ tsp dried thyme
1 garlic clove, finely chopped
350 g/12 oz/1$^3/_4$ cups arborio or
  carnaroli rice
1.2 litres/2 pints/5 cups chicken or
  vegetable stock, simmering

4 cooked beetroot (not in vinegar),
  diced
2 tbsp chopped fresh dill
2 tbsp fresh snipped chives
salt and pepper
60 g/2 oz/$^2/_3$ cup freshly grated
  Parmesan cheese, to serve (optional)

1 Put the sour cherries in a saucepan with the wine and bring to the boil, then simmer for 2–3 minutes until slightly reduced. Remove from the heat and set aside.

2 Heat the olive oil in a large heavy-based saucepan over a medium heat. Add the onion, celery and thyme and cook for about 2 minutes until just beginning to soften. Add the garlic and rice and cook, stirring, until the rice is well coated.

3 Add a ladleful (about 225 ml/8 fl oz/1 cup) of the simmering stock; it will bubble and steam rapidly. Cook, stirring constantly, until the stock is absorbed.

4 Continue adding the stock, about half a ladleful at a time, allowing each addition to be absorbed before adding the next – never allow the rice to cook 'dry'. This should take 20–25 minutes. The risotto should have a creamy consistency and the rice should be tender, but firm to the bite.

5 Half way through the cooking time, remove the cherries from the wine with a slotted spoon and add to the risotto with the beetroot and half the wine. Continue adding the stock or remaining wine.

6 Stir in the dill and chives and season, if necessary. Serve with the Parmesan, if wished.

Courgette (Zucchini) & Basil Risotto

*An easy way of livening up a simple risotto is to use a flavoured olive oil –
here a basil-flavoured oil heightens the taste of the dish.*

Serves 4–6

INGREDIENTS

4 tbsp basil-flavoured extra-virgin
  olive oil, plus extra for drizzling
4 courgettes (zucchini), diced
1 yellow (bell) pepper, cored, deseeded
  and diced
2 garlic cloves, finely chopped
1 large onion, finely chopped

400 g/14 oz/2 cups arborio or
  carnaroli rice
60 ml/3 fl oz/⅓ cup dry white
  vermouth
1.5 litres/2¾ pints/6¼ cups chicken or
  vegetable stock, simmering

25 g/1 oz/2 tbsp unsalted butter, at
  room temperature
large handful of fresh basil leaves,
  torn, plus a few leaves to garnish
80 g/3 oz/1 cup freshly grated
  Parmesan cheese

1 Heat half the oil in a large frying pan (skillet) over high heat. When very hot, but not smoking, add the courgettes (zucchini) and yellow (bell) pepper and stir-fry for 3 minutes until lightly golden. Stir in the garlic and cook for about 30 seconds longer. Transfer to a plate and set aside.

2 Heat the remaining oil in a large heavy-based saucepan over a medium heat. Add the chopped onion and cook for about 2 minutes until softened. Add the rice and cook, stirring frequently, for about 2 minutes until the rice is translucent and well coated with the oil.

3 Pour in the vermouth; it will bubble and steam rapidly and evaporate almost immediately. Add a ladleful (about 225 ml/8 fl oz/1 cup) of the simmering stock and cook, stirring constantly until the stock is absorbed.

4 Continue adding the stock, about half a ladleful at a time, allowing each addition to be absorbed before adding the next. This should take 20–25 minutes. The risotto should have a creamy consistency and the rice should be tender, but still firm to the bite.

5 Stir in the courgette (zucchini) mixture with any juices, the butter, basil and Parmesan. Drizzle with a little oil and garnish with basil. Serve hot.

Wild Rocket (Arugula) & Tomato Risotto with Mozzarella

It's worth searching around for wild rocket as its robust peppery flavour makes all the difference to this dish. Teamed with vine-ripened plum tomatoes and real buffalo mozzarella, this risotto is sensational.

Serves 4–6

INGREDIENTS

2 tbsp olive oil
25 g/1 oz/2 tbsp unsalted butter
1 large onion, finely chopped
2 garlic cloves, finely chopped
350 g/12 oz/1¾ cups arborio rice
120 ml/4 fl oz/½ cup dry white vermouth (optional)

1.5 litres/2¾ pints/6¼ cups chicken or vegetable stock, simmering
6 vine-ripened or Italian plum tomatoes, deseeded and chopped
125 g/4½ oz wild rocket (arugula)
handful of fresh basil leaves

115 g/4 oz/1⅓ cups freshly grated Parmesan cheese
225 g/8 oz fresh Italian buffalo mozzarella, coarsely grated or diced
salt and pepper

1 Heat the oil and half the butter in a large frying pan (skillet). Add the onion and cook for about 2 minutes until just beginning to soften. Stir in the garlic and rice and cook, stirring frequently, until the rice is translucent and well coated.

2 Pour in the white vermouth, if using; it will bubble and steam rapidly and evaporate almost immediately. Add a ladleful (about 225 ml/8 fl oz/1 cup) of the simmering stock and cook, stirring constantly, until it is absorbed.

3 Continue adding the stock, about half a ladleful at a time, allowing each addition to be absorbed before adding the next – never allow the rice to cook 'dry'.

4 Just before the rice is tender, stir in the chopped tomatoes and rocket (arugula). Shred the basil leaves and immediately stir into the risotto. Continue to cook, adding more stock, until the risotto is creamy and the rice is tender, but firm to the bite.

5 Remove from the heat and stir in the remaining butter, the Parmesan and mozzarella. Season to taste with salt and pepper. Cover and stand for about 1 minute. Serve immediately, before the mozzarella melts completely.

Risotto with Sun-dried Tomatoes & Pecorino

Pecorino is an Italian cheese made from sheep's milk. Although it is made and used all over Italy, the aged pecorino from Sardinia – pecorino sardo – is particularly good for this dish.

Serves 6

INGREDIENTS

about 12 sun-dried tomatoes, not in oil

2 tbsp olive oil

1 large onion, finely chopped

4–6 garlic cloves, finely chopped

400 g/14 oz/2 cups arborio or carnaroli rice

1.5 litres/2¾ pints/6¼ cups chicken or vegetable stock, simmering

2 tbsp chopped fresh flat-leaf parsley

115 g/4 oz/1 cup grated aged pecorino cheese

extra-virgin olive oil, for drizzling

1 Place the sun-dried tomatoes in a bowl and pour over enough boiling water to cover. Stand for about 30 minutes until soft and supple. Drain and pat dry, then shred thinly and set aside.

2 Heat the oil in a heavy-based saucepan over a medium heat. Add the onion and cook for about 2 minutes until beginning to soften. Add the garlic and cook for 15 seconds. Add the rice and cook, stirring frequently, for 2 minutes until the rice is translucent and well coated with oil.

3 Add a ladleful (about 225 ml/8 fl oz/1 cup) of the hot stock; the stock will bubble and steam rapidly. Cook, stirring constantly, until the liquid is absorbed.

4 Continue adding the stock, about half a ladleful at a time, allowing each addition to be absorbed before adding the next – never allow the rice to cook 'dry'.

5 After about 15 minutes, stir in the sun-dried tomatoes. Continue to cook, adding the stock, until the rice is tender, but firm to the bite. The risotto should have a creamy consistency.

6 Remove from the heat and stir in the parsley and half the cheese. Cover, stand for about 1 minute, then spoon into serving dishes. Drizzle with extra-virgin olive oil and sprinkle the remaining cheese over the top. Serve immediately.

Orange-scented Risotto

This fragrant risotto makes a delicate first course for a special meal.
Serve with a sprinkling of grated Parmesan, if wished.

Serves 4

INGREDIENTS

2 tbsp pine kernels (nuts)
60 g/2 oz/4 tbsp unsalted butter
2 shallots, finely chopped
1 leek, finely shredded

400 g/14 oz/2 cups arborio or
   carnaroli rice
2 tbsp orange-flavoured liqueur or
   dry white vermouth
1.5 litres/2¾ pint/6¼ cups chicken or
   vegetable stock, simmering

grated rind of 1 orange
juice of 2 oranges, strained
3 tbsp snipped fresh chives
salt and pepper

1 Toast the pine kernels (nuts) in a frying pan (skillet) over a medium heat for about 3 minutes, stirring and shaking frequently, until golden brown. Set aside.

2 Heat half the butter in a large heavy-based saucepan over a medium heat. Add the shallots and leek and cook for about 2 minutes until they begin to soften. Add the rice and cook, stirring frequently, for about 2 minutes until the rice is translucent and well coated with the butter.

3 Pour in the liqueur or vermouth; it will bubble and steam rapidly and evaporate almost immediately. Add a ladleful (about 225 ml/8 fl oz/1 cup) of the hot stock and cook, stirring, until absorbed.

4 Continue adding the stock, about half a ladleful at a time, allowing each addition to be absorbed before adding the next – never allow the rice to cook 'dry'.

5 After about 15 minutes, add the orange rind and juice and continue to cook, adding more

stock, until the rice is tender, but firm to the bite. The risotto should have a creamy consistency.

6 Remove from the heat and stir in the remaining butter and 2 tablespoons of the chives. Season with salt and pepper. Spoon into serving dishes and sprinkle with the toasted pine kernels (nuts) and the remaining chives.

Black Cherry Risotto

This risotto is flavoured like a rice pilaf, using cherries and almonds.
It has a delicious fruity yet tangy flavour.

Serves 6

INGREDIENTS

2 tbsp unblanched almonds

2 tbsp sunflower or vegetable oil

1 red onion, finely chopped

2 tbsp dried sour cherries or raisins

450 g/1 lb black cherries or small black plums, stoned (pitted) and halved

350 g/12 oz/1¾ cups arborio or carnaroli rice

225 ml/8 fl oz/1 cup port or fruity red wine

1.2 litres/2 pints/5 cups chicken or vegetable stock, simmering

50 ml/2 fl oz/¼ cup double (heavy) cream (optional)

2 tbsp chopped fresh chives, plus whole chives for garnishing

salt and pepper

1 Lightly toast the almonds in a frying pan (skillet) for about 2 minutes until golden. Cool, then chop coarsely. Set aside.

2 Heat the oil in a large heavy-based saucepan over a medium heat. Add the onion and cook, stirring frequently, for about 2 minutes until beginning to soften. Add the dried cherries and the black cherries and stir for 2–3 minutes until the cherries begin to soften. Add the rice to the pan and cook, stirring frequently, until the rice is translucent and well coated.

3 Pour in the port; it will bubble and steam rapidly. Cook, stirring, until it is absorbed. Add a ladleful (about 225 ml/8 fl oz/1 cup) of the simmering stock and cook, stirring constantly until the stock is absorbed.

4 Continue adding the stock, about half a ladleful at a time, allowing each addition to be absorbed before adding the next – never allow the rice to cook 'dry'. This should take 20–25 minutes. The risotto should have a creamy consistency and the rice should be tender, but still firm to the bite.

5 Stir in the cream, if using, and season with salt and pepper. Remove from the heat, stir in the chives and spoon into serving bowls. Sprinkle with the chopped almonds, garnish with the chives and serve immediately.

Crab Risotto with Roasted (Bell) Peppers

A different way to make the most of crab,
this rich-tasting and colourful risotto is full of interesting flavours.

Serves 4–6

INGREDIENTS

2–3 large red (bell) peppers
3 tbsp olive oil
1 onion, finely chopped
1 small fennel bulb, finely chopped
2 stalks celery, finely chopped
¼–½ tsp cayenne pepper, or to taste

350 g/12 oz/1¾ cups arborio or
  carnaroli rice
800 g/1 lb 12 oz can Italian peeled
  plum tomatoes, drained and
  chopped
50 ml/2 fl oz/¼ cup dry white
  vermouth (optional)

1.5 litres/2¾ pints/6¼ cups fish or
  light chicken stock, simmering
450 g/1 lb fresh cooked crab meat
  (white and dark meat)
50 ml/2 fl oz/¼ cup lemon juice
2–4 tbsp chopped fresh parsley or chervil
salt and pepper

1 Grill (broil) the (bell) peppers until the skins are charred. Transfer to a plastic bag and twist to seal. When cool enough to handle, peel off the charred skins, working over a bowl to catch the juices. Remove the cores and seeds; chop the flesh and set aside, reserving the juices.

2 Heat the olive oil in a large heavy-based saucepan. Add the onion, fennel and celery and cook for 2–3 minutes until the vegetables are softened. Add the cayenne and rice and cook, stirring frequently, for about 2 minutes until the rice is translucent and well coated.

3 Stir in the tomatoes and vermouth, if using. The liquid will bubble and steam rapidly. When the liquid is almost absorbed, add a ladleful (about 225 ml/8 fl oz/ 1 cup) of the simmering stock. Cook, stirring constantly, until the liquid is completely absorbed.

4 Continue adding the stock, about half a ladleful at a time, allowing each addition to be absorbed before adding the next. This should take 20–25 minutes. The risotto should have a creamy consistency and the rice should be tender, but firm to the bite.

5 Stir in the red (bell) peppers and juices, the crab meat, lemon juice and parsley or chervil and heat. Season with salt and pepper to taste. Serve immediately.

Risotto with Clams

This simple recipe is an excellent way of using the tiny Venus clams when they are in season. The tomatoes add a splash of colour.

Serves 6

INGREDIENTS

50 ml/2 fl oz/¼ cup olive oil
1 large onion, finely chopped
2 kg/4 lb 8 oz tiny clams, such as
   Venus, well scrubbed
120 ml/4 fl oz/½ cup dry white wine
1 litre/1¾ pints/4 cups fish stock

600 ml/1 pint/2½ cups water
3 garlic cloves, finely chopped
½ tsp crushed dried chilli (or to taste)
400 g/14 oz/2 cups arborio or
   carnaroli rice

3 ripe plum tomatoes, skinned and
   coarsely chopped
3 tbsp lemon juice
2 tbsp chopped fresh chervil or parsley
salt and pepper

1 Heat 1–2 tablespoons of the oil in a large heavy-based saucepan over a medium-high heat. Add the onion and stir-fry for about 1 minute. Add the clams and wine and cover tightly. Cook for 2–3 minutes, shaking the pan frequently, until the clams begin to open. Remove from the heat and discard any clams that do not open.

2 When cool enough to handle, remove the clams from their shells. Rinse in the cooking liquid. Cover the clams and set aside.

Strain the cooking liquid through a paper coffee filter or a sieve lined with a paper towel and reserve.

3 Bring the fish stock and water to the boil in a saucepan, then reduce the heat and keep at a gentle simmer.

4 Heat the remaining olive oil in a large, heavy-based saucepan over a medium heat. Add the garlic and chilli and cook gently for 1 minute. Add the rice and cook, stirring frequently, for

about 2 minutes until translucent and well coated with oil.

5 Add a ladleful (about 225 ml/8 fl oz/1 cup) of the simmering stock mixture; it will bubble and steam rapidly. Cook, stirring constantly, until the liquid is completely absorbed.

6 Continue adding the stock, about half a ladleful at a time, allowing each addition to be absorbed before adding the next – never allow the rice to cook 'dry'. This should take 20–25 minutes. The risotto should have a creamy consistency and the rice should be tender, but firm to the bite.

7 Stir in the tomatoes, reserved clams and their cooking liquid, the lemon juice and chervil. Heat through. Season to taste and serve immediately.

Black Risotto

*This classic recipe gets its name from the squid ink which turns the
risotto 'black'. A sophisticated dish, sure to impress.*

Serves 6

INGREDIENTS

2–3 tbsp olive oil

450 g/1 lb cleaned squid or cuttlefish,
    cut crossways into thin strips, rinsed
    and patted dry

2 tbsp lemon juice

25 g/1 oz/2 tbsp unsalted butter

3–4 garlic cloves, finely chopped

1 tsp crushed dried chilli, or to taste

350 g/12 oz/1¾ cups arborio or
    carnaroli rice

120 ml/4 fl oz/½ cup dry white wine

1 litre/l¾ pints/4 cups fish stock,
    simmering

2 sachets squid or cuttlefish ink

2 tbsp chopped fresh flat-leaf parsley

salt and pepper

1 Heat half the olive oil in a
large heavy-based frying pan
(skillet) over a medium-high heat.
When the oil is very hot, add the
squid strips and stir-fry for 2–3
minutes until just cooked.
Transfer to a plate and sprinkle
with the lemon juice.

2 Heat the remaining olive
oil and butter in a large
heavy-based pan over a medium
heat. Add the garlic and chilli and
cook gently for 1 minute. Add the
rice and cook, stirring frequently,
for about 2 minutes until
translucent and well coated.

3 Pour in the white wine; it will
bubble and steam rapidly.
Cook, stirring frequently, until the
wine is completely absorbed by the
rice. Add a ladleful (about 225 ml/
8 fl oz/1 cup) of the simmering fish
stock and cook, stirring constantly,
until it is completely absorbed.

4 Continue adding the stock,
about half a ladleful at a time,
allowing each addition to be
absorbed before adding the next –
never allow the rice to cook 'dry'.
This should take 20–25 minutes.
The risotto should have a creamy
consistency and the rice should be
tender, but firm to the bite.

5 Just before adding the last
ladleful of stock, add the squid
ink to the stock and stir to blend
completely. Stir into the risotto
with the reserved squid pieces and
the parsley. Season with salt and
pepper to taste. Serve immediately.

Rich Lobster Risotto

Although lobster is expensive, this dish is worth it.
Keeping it simple allows the lobster flavour to come through.

Serves 4

INGREDIENTS

1 tbsp vegetable oil
60 g/2 oz/4 tbsp unsalted butter
2 shallots, finely chopped
300 g/10½ oz/1½ cups arborio or
  carnaroli rice
½ tsp cayenne pepper, or to taste

80 ml/3 fl oz/⅓ cup dry white
  vermouth
1.5 litres/2¾ pints/6¼ cups shellfish,
  fish or light chicken stock,
  simmering
225 g/8 oz cherry tomatoes, quartered
  and deseeded

2–3 tbsp double (heavy) or whipping
  cream
450 g/1 lb/about 2 cups cooked
  lobster meat, cut into coarse chunks
2 tbsp chopped fresh chervil or dill
salt and white pepper

1 Heat the oil and half the butter in a large heavy-based saucepan over a medium heat. Add the shallots and cook for about 2 minutes until just beginning to soften. Add the rice and cayenne pepper and cook, stirring frequently, for about 2 minutes until the rice is translucent and well coated with the oil and butter.

2 Pour in the vermouth; it will bubble and steam rapidly and evaporate almost immediately.

3 Add a ladleful (about 225 ml/8 fl oz/1 cup) of the simmering stock and cook, stirring constantly, until the stock is absorbed.

4 Continue adding the stock, about half a ladleful at a time, allowing each addition to be absorbed before adding the next – never allow the rice to cook 'dry'. This should take 20–25 minutes. The risotto should have a creamy consistency and the rice should be tender, but firm to the bite.

5 Stir in the tomatoes and cream and cook for about 2 minutes.

6 Add the cooked lobster meat, with the remaining butter and chervil, and cook long enough to just heat the lobster meat gently. Serve immediately.

Radicchio Risotto with Pancetta & Cream

In this risotto, the slightly bitter flavour of radicchio is balanced by the addition of sweet double (heavy) cream, while pancetta provides a subtle smoky contrast.

Serves 6–8

INGREDIENTS

1 large head radicchio, outer damaged leaves removed
2 tbsp sunflower or other vegetable oil
25 g/1 oz/2 tbsp unsalted butter
115 g/4 oz pancetta or thick-cut smoky bacon, diced
1 large onion, finely chopped

1 garlic clove, finely chopped
400 g/14 oz/2 cups arborio or carnaroli rice
1 .5 litres/2¾ pints/6¼ cups chicken or vegetable stock, simmering
50 ml/2 fl oz/¼ cup double (heavy) cream

60 g/2 oz/⅔ cup freshly grated Parmesan cheese
3–4 tbsp chopped fresh flat-leaf parsley
salt and pepper
fresh flat-leaf parsley sprigs, to garnish

1 Cut the radicchio head in half lengthways; remove the triangular core. Place the halves cut-side down and shred finely. Set aside.

2 Heat the oil and butter in a heavy-based pan over a medium-high heat. Add the diced pancetta and cook for 3–4 minutes, stirring occasionally, until it begins to colour. Add the onion and garlic and cook for 1 minute, or until just beginning to soften.

3 Add the rice and cook, stirring frequently, for 2 minutes until translucent and well coated with the oil and butter. Stir in the radicchio for 1 minute until just beginning to wilt. Reduce the heat to medium.

4 Add a ladleful (about 225 ml/8 fl oz/1 cup) of the simmering stock; the stock will bubble and steam rapidly. Cook, stirring constantly, until the stock is completely absorbed.

5 Continue adding the stock, about half a ladleful at a time, allowing each addition to be absorbed before adding the next. This should take 20–25 minutes. The risotto should have a creamy consistency and the rice should be tender, but firm to the bite.

6 Stir in the cream, Parmesan and parsley. Season with salt and pepper. Remove from the heat. Cover and stand for 1 minute. Garnish with parsley and serve.

Italian Sausage & Rosemary Risotto

This recipe is made with a mild Italian sausage called luganega, *but you can use any sausage you like – sweet fennel sausage, a very spicy Italian sausage or even a Spanish chorizo would produce a good result.*

Serves 4–6

INGREDIENTS

2 long sprigs fresh rosemary, plus
  extra to garnish
2 tbsp olive oil
60 g/2 oz/4 tbsp unsalted butter
1 large onion, finely chopped
1 stalk celery, finely chopped
2 garlic cloves, finely chopped

1/2 tsp dried thyme leaves
450 g/1 lb pork sausage such as
  luganega or Cumberland, cut into
  1 cm/1/2 inch pieces
350 g/12 oz/1 3/4 cups arborio or
  carnaroli rice
120 ml/4 fl oz/1/2 cup fruity red wine

1.3 litres/2 1/4 pints/5 2/3 cups chicken
  stock, simmering
80 g/3 oz/1 cup freshly grated
  Parmesan cheese
salt and pepper

1 Strip the long thin leaves from the rosemary sprigs and chop finely; set aside.

2 Heat the oil and half the butter in a large heavy-based saucepan over a medium heat. Add the onion and celery and cook for about 2 minutes. Stir in the garlic, thyme, sausage and rosemary. Cook for about 5 minutes, stirring frequently, until the sausage begins to brown. Transfer the sausage to a plate.

3 Stir the rice into the pan and cook for about 2 minutes until the grains are translucent and coated with the butter and oil.

4 Pour in the red wine; it will bubble and steam rapidly and evaporate almost immediately. Add a ladleful (about 225 ml/8 fl oz/1 cup) of the simmering stock and cook, stirring, until it is absorbed.

5 Continue adding the stock, about half a ladleful at a time,

allowing each addition to be absorbed before adding the next. This should take 20–25 minutes. The risotto should have a creamy consistency and the rice should be tender, but firm to the bite.

6 Return the sausage pieces to the risotto and heat through. Remove from the heat; stir in the remaining butter and Parmesan. Season with salt and pepper. Cover, stand for about 1 minute, then garnish with rosemary. Serve.

Arrancini

These little risotto-ball snacks are as popular in New York as they are in Rome.
The mozzarella centres ooze deliciously when you bite into them.

Serves 6–8

INGREDIENTS

1 quantity Easy Cheesy Risotto
   with Parmesan (see page 100),
   completely cooled
3 eggs
3 tbsp chopped fresh flat-leaf parsley

115 g/4 oz/²⁄₃ cup mozzarella, diced
vegetable oil, for frying
about 80 g/3 oz/²⁄₃ cup plain
   (all-purpose) flour

about 100 g/3¹⁄₂ oz/l¹⁄₂ cups dried
   breadcrumbs, preferably homemade
salt and pepper

1 Put the risotto in a large mixing bowl and stir to break up. Beat 2 of the eggs lightly, then gradually beat enough into the risotto until the risotto begins to stick together. Beat in the parsley.

2 Using wet hands, form the mixture into balls about the size of a large egg.

3 Poke a hole in the centre of each ball and fill with a few cubes of the mozzarella. Carefully seal the hole over with the risotto mixture. Place on a large baking (cookie) sheet.

4 In a deep-fat fryer or large heavy-based saucepan, heat about 7.5 cm/3 inches of oil to 180–190°C/350-375°F or until a cube of bread browns.

5 Spread the flour on a large plate and season with salt and pepper. In a small bowl, beat the remaining egg and add any unused egg from Step 1. Spread the breadcrumbs on another large plate and season with salt and pepper.

6 Roll each risotto ball in a little seasoned flour, shaking off the excess. Carefully coat in the egg,

then roll in the breadcrumbs to coat completely.

7 Deep fry 3–4 balls for about 2 minutes until crisp and golden, then transfer to paper towels to drain. Keep hot in a warm oven while frying the remaining balls. Serve immediately while the cheese is still soft and melted.

Frittata Risotto

*An excellent way of using up leftover risotto, this fried risotto 'cake' makes a great first course,
or a tasty accompaniment to roasted or grilled (broiled) meats.*

Serves 4–6

INGREDIENTS

about 80 ml/3 fl oz/⅓ cup olive oil
1 large red onion, finely chopped
1 red (bell) pepper, cored, deseeded
and chopped
1 garlic clove, finely chopped

3-4 sun-dried tomatoes, finely
shredded
2 tbsp chopped fresh flat-leaf parsley
or basil

1 quantity Easy Cheesy Risotto with
Parmesan (see page 100) or Risotto
alla Milanese (see page 156), cooled
about 60 g/2 oz/⅔ cup freshly grated
Parmesan cheese

1 Heat 2 tablespoons of the oil in a large heavy-based frying pan (skillet) over a medium-high heat. Add the onion and red (bell) pepper and cook for 3–4 minutes until the vegetables are soft.

2 Add the garlic and sun-dried tomatoes and cook for 2 minutes. Remove from the heat. Stir in the parsley; cool slightly.

3 Put the risotto in a bowl and break up with a fork. Stir in the vegetable mixture with half the Parmesan. Stir to mix well.

4 Reserve 1 tablespoon of the remaining oil and heat the rest in the cleaned frying pan (skillet) over a medium heat. Remove from the heat and spoon in the risotto mixture, pressing it into an even cake-like layer, about 2–2.5 cm/¾–1 inch thick. Return to the heat and cook for about 4 minutes until crisp and brown on the bottom.

5 With a palette knife, loosen the edges and give the pan a shake. Slide the frittata on to a large plate. Protecting your hands,

invert the frying pan (skillet) over the frittata and, holding both firmly together, flip them over. Return to the heat and drizzle the remaining oil around the edge of the frittata, gently pulling the edges towards the centre with the palette knife. Cook for 1–2 minutes to seal the bottom, then slide on to a serving plate.

6 Sprinkle the top with some of the remaining Parmesan. Cut into wedges and serve with the rest of the Parmesan.

Cheese-topped Risotto Tart with Spinach

Risotto, combined with spinach and cheese, makes a mouthwatering filling for this tart. If preferred, you can use six 10 cm/4 inch individual tart tins (pans) instead of a large one.

Serves 6–8

INGREDIENTS

185 g/6½ oz/1⅔ cups plain (all-purpose) flour
½ tsp salt
1 tsp caster (superfine) sugar
115 g/4 oz/½ cup unsalted butter, diced

1 egg yolk, beaten with 2 tbsp iced water

FILLING:
1 quantity Easy Cheesy Risotto with Parmesan (see page 100), still warm

250 g/9 oz spinach, cooked, drained very well and chopped
2 tbsp double (heavy) cream
225 g/8 oz mozzarella, preferably buffalo
80 g/3 oz/1 cup freshly grated Parmesan cheese

1 To make the shortcrust pastry sift the flour, salt and sugar into a large bowl and sprinkle over the butter. Rub the butter into the flour until the mixture forms coarse crumbs. Sprinkle in the egg mixture and stir to make a dough.

2 Gather the dough into a ball, wrap in cling film (plastic wrap) and chill for at least 1 hour.

3 Gently roll out the pastry (piecrust) to a thickness of about 3 mm/⅛ inch, then use to line a lightly greased 23–25 cm/9–10 inch tart tin (pan) with a removable base. Prick the bottom with a fork and chill for 1 hour.

4 Cover the tart case with baking parchment and fill with baking beans. Bake blind in a preheated oven at 200°C/400°F/Gas Mark 6 for about 20 minutes until the pastry (piecrust) is set and the edge is golden. Remove the beans and parchment and set aside.

Reduce the oven temperature to 180°C/350°F/ Gas Mark 4.

5 Put the risotto in a bowl and stir in the spinach, cream, half the mozzarella and half the Parmesan. Spoon into the tart case and smooth the top. Sprinkle evenly with the remaining cheeses.

6 Bake for 12–15 minutes or until cooked through and golden. Cool slightly on a wire rack, then serve warm.

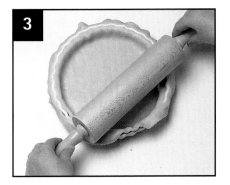

Oven-baked Risotto with Mushrooms

This easy-to-make risotto is a good choice for entertaining as it eliminates the need for constant stirring. The result is creamy and moist – more like a rice pudding.

Serves 4–6

INGREDIENTS

4 tbsp olive oil
400 g/14 oz portobello or large field
   mushrooms, thickly sliced
115 g/4 oz pancetta or thick-cut
   smoky bacon, diced
1 large onion, finely chopped

2 garlic cloves, finely chopped
350 g/12 oz/1¾ cups arborio or
   carnaroli rice
1.2 litres/2 pints/5 cups chicken stock,
   simmering

2 tbsp chopped fresh tarragon or flat-
   leaf parsley
80 g/3 oz/1 cup freshly grated
   Parmesan cheese, plus extra for
   sprinkling
salt and pepper

1 Heat 2 tablespoons of the oil in a large heavy-based frying pan (skillet) over a high heat. Add the mushrooms and stir-fry for 2–3 minutes until golden and tender-crisp. Transfer to a plate.

2 Add the pancetta to the pan and cook for about 2 minutes, stirring frequently, until crisp and golden. Add to the mushrooms on the plate.

3 Heat the remaining oil in a heavy-based saucepan over a medium heat. Add the onion and cook for about 2 minutes until beginning to soften. Add the garlic and rice and cook, stirring, for about 2 minutes until the rice is well coated with the oil.

4 Gradually stir the stock into the rice, then add the mushroom and pancetta mixture and the tarragon. Season with salt and pepper. Bring to the boil.

5 Remove from the heat and transfer to a casserole.

6 Cover and bake in a preheated oven at 180°C/350°F/Gas Mark 4 for about 20 minutes until the rice is almost tender and most of the liquid is absorbed. Uncover and stir in the Parmesan. Continue to bake for about 15 minutes longer until the rice is tender, but still firm to the bite. Serve at once with extra Parmesan for sprinkling.

Famous Rice Dishes

In this chapter, you can travel the world and sample some of the traditional and delectable rice dishes that have evolved in the various rice-producing countries over hundreds of years, using a blend of exotic flavours and ingredients.

For a flavour of Europe, try your hand at making a Spanish Paella, a wonderful mix of chicken, shellfish and rice, or serve the delicately flavoured Greek Egg & Lemon Soup as a light lunch. Travelling to the Middle East, savour an unusual, spicy lamb and rice sausage, Mumbar, or learn how to make delicious Mujadarah, a marvellous combination of rice, lentils and caramelized onions.

Capture the exotic flavours of India with Murgh Pullau, a fragrant chicken and almond pilaf, or discover the delights of Thai cooking with spicy red pork curry with jasmine-scented rice. Popular Chinese Fried Rice is a must to try at home and the classic fried rice dish of Indonesia, Nasi Goreng, a medley of Far-Eastern flavours, is ideal for any occasion. Vietnamese Spring Rolls are a culinary treat and fun to eat, while for entertaining, Japanese Sushi make stunning fare.

Risotto alla Milanese

This risotto, traditionally served as an accompaniment to Ossobuco alla Milanese,
is one of the world's most beautiful and elegant dishes.

Serves 4–6

INGREDIENTS

¹/₂–1 tsp saffron threads
1.3 litres/2¹/₄ pints/5²/₃ cups chicken
   stock, simmering
80 g/3 oz/6 tbsp unsalted butter

2–3 shallots, finely chopped
400 g/14 oz/2 cups arborio or
   carnaroli rice

175 g/6 oz/2 cups freshly grated
   Parmesan cheese
salt and pepper

1 Put the saffron threads in a small bowl. Pour over enough of the stock to cover the threads, then set aside to infuse.

2 Melt 25 g/1 oz/2 tablespoons of the butter in a large heavy-based pan over a medium heat. Add the shallots and cook for about 2 minutes until beginning to soften. Add the rice and cook, stirring frequently, for about 2 minutes until the rice is beginning to turn translucent and is well coated.

3 Add a ladleful (about 225 ml/8 fl oz/1 cup) of the simmering stock; it will steam and bubble rapidly. Cook, stirring constantly, until the liquid is absorbed.

4 Continue adding the stock, about half a ladleful at a time, allowing each addition to be absorbed before adding the next – never allow the rice to cook 'dry'.

5 After about 15 minutes, stir in the saffron-infused stock; the rice will turn a vibrant yellow and the colour will become deeper as it cooks. Continue cooking, adding the stock in the same way until the rice is tender, but still firm to the bite. The risotto should have a creamy porridge-like consistency.

6 Stir in the remaining butter and half the Parmesan, then remove from the heat. Cover and stand for about 1 minute.

7 Spoon the risotto into serving bowls and serve immediately with the remaining Parmesan.

Dolmades

These stuffed grape-vine leaves are popular all over the Middle-East, where they are served as part of a meze – a selection of appetizers. This is a simple rice version.

Serves 10–12

INGREDIENTS

115 g/4 oz/about 24 large vine leaves, packed in brine, drained

olive oil

1 onion, finely chopped

2 garlic cloves, finely chopped

3/4 tsp dried thyme

3/4 tsp dried oregano

1/2 tsp ground cinnamon

200 g/7 oz/1 cup long-grain white rice

350 ml/12 fl oz/1 1/2 cups water

2 tsp raisins

2 tbsp pine kernels (nuts), lightly toasted

2 tbsp chopped fresh mint

1 tbsp chopped fresh flat-leaf parsley

4 tbsp lemon juice

350 ml/12 fl oz/1 1/2 cups chicken stock

salt and pepper

1 Cover the vine leaves with boiling water and leave for 2 minutes. Drain, rinse and pat dry. Cut off any thick stems. Place shiny-side down on paper towels.

2 Heat 2 tablespoons of the olive oil in a heavy-based pan. Add the onion and cook for about 3 minutes until soft. Stir in the garlic, dried herbs and cinnamon, then add the rice and cook for about 2 minutes, stirring, until translucent and coated with the oil.

3 Stir in the water and raisins and bring to the boil, stirring twice. Simmer, covered tightly, for 15 minutes until the liquid is absorbed and the rice just tender.

4 Fork the rice into a bowl and add the pine kernels (nuts), mint, parsley and half the lemon juice. Stir and season with salt and pepper and 1 tablespoon olive oil.

5 Place about 1 tablespoon of the rice mixture on a vine leaf near the stem end and roll the leaf once over the filling. Fold in each side of the leaf, then finish rolling. Repeat with the remaining leaves.

6 Brush a large deep flameproof dish or casserole with about 2 tablespoons of olive oil. Arrange the dolmades tightly in 2 rows, making a second layer if necessary. Sprinkle with another tablespoon of the oil and the remaining lemon juice. Add the stock to cover the rolls; add extra water if necessary to make enough liquid.

7 Weight down the rolls with a heatproof plate, cover tightly with a lid or kitchen foil and cook over a very low heat for about 1 hour. Remove from the heat and allow to cool to room temperature. Drain and serve with a little of the cooking juices, if wished.

Mujadarah

*This delicious combination of rice, lentils and caramelized onions
is often served as part of a Lebanese meze.*

Serves 6

INGREDIENTS

225 g/8 oz/1 cup green or brown
   lentils, rinsed
120 m/4 fl oz/¹/₂ cup olive oil
3 large onions, thinly sliced
200 g/7 oz/1 cup basmati or long-
   grain white rice

700 ml/1¹/₄ pints/3 cups light chicken
   or vegetable stock
1 tsp ground allspice or ground
   cinnamon
salt and pepper

TO SERVE:
lemon wedges
spring onions (scallions), thinly sliced
   on the diagonal
natural yogurt

1 Bring a large saucepan of water to the boil. Gradually pour in the lentils (so the water remains boiling). Reduce the heat to medium-low and simmer for about 25 minutes, skimming off any foam that rises to the surface, until just tender. Drain the lentils and set aside (see Cook's Tip).

2 Meanwhile, heat the oil in a large, deep frying pan (skillet) over a medium heat until very hot. Add the onions and cook for 4–5 minutes until soft. Using a slotted spoon, transfer about two-thirds of the onions to a bowl; set aside. Continue cooking the remaining onions until brown and crisp, then drain on a paper towel.

3 Add the rice to the pan and cook, stirring frequently, for about 2 minutes until translucent and well coated with the oil. Add the less-cooked onions, with the lentils and stock and stir gently, scraping the base of the pan to release any crispy bits. Add the ground allspice and season with salt and pepper.

4 Tightly cover the pan and cook over a very low heat for about 20 minutes until the rice is tender and all the stock is absorbed. Fork the rice mixture into a serving bowl; top with the crispy onions. Serve with lemon wedges, spring onions (scallions) and yogurt.

COOK'S TIP

*If preferred, reserve the lentil
cooking liquid and use instead of
the chicken or vegetable stock.*

Greek Egg & Lemon Soup

The rice not only adds texture to this soup, but also helps to thicken the broth slightly.
Add the egg and lemon mixture carefully as the soup can easily curdle.

Serves 6–8

INGREDIENTS

1.5 litres/2³⁄₄ pints/6¹⁄₄ cups chicken
   or lamb stock
75–100 g/2³⁄₄–3¹⁄₂ oz/¹⁄₃–¹⁄₂ cup long-
   grain white rice

3 eggs, separated
3–4 tbsp lemon juice
1 tbsp water

salt and white pepper
1 tbsp chopped fresh flat-leaf
   parsley, to garnish (optional)

1 Bring the stock to the boil in a large saucepan. Add the rice in a very slow stream so the stock does not stop boiling; stir once or twice. Reduce the heat and simmer gently, partially covered, until the rice is tender; skim off any foam which rises to the surface.

2 Whisk the egg whites in a large bowl until almost stiff.

3 Add the egg yolks and continue whisking until the mixture is light and creamy. Gradually beat in the lemon juice and water.

4 Gradually whisk in half of the hot stock and rice, about 2 tablespoons at a time. Be careful to add the hot stock very slowly to the egg and lemon mixture, and whisk constantly, otherwise the eggs may curdle.

5 Remove the remaining stock and rice from the heat, transfer to a bowl and gradually whisk in the egg and stock mixture. Continue to whisk for 1 minute to allow the stock to cool slightly. Season with salt and pepper and serve immediately. Garnish with a little chopped parsley, if wished.

COOK'S TIP

Using a food processor can help prevent the egg and lemon mixture from curdling. Add the egg whites to a food processor fitted with the metal blade and process for about 1 minute until very thick and foamy. Add the egg yolks and continue to process for 1 minute. With the machine running, gradually pour the lemon and water through the feed tube until combined. Continue from Step 4.

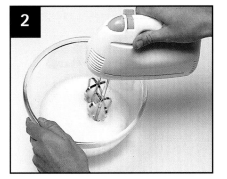

Kedgeree

Originally served at Victorian breakfast tables, kedgeree probably derives from an Indian dish called khichri. The strong flavour of the smoked fish is a perfect match for the blandness of rice.

Serves 4–6

INGREDIENTS

700 g/1½ lb thick, undyed smoked
   haddock or cod fillets
milk, for poaching
2 bay leaves
1 tbsp vegetable oil
60 g/2 oz/4 tbsp butter
1 onion, finely chopped

1 tsp hot curry powder, or to taste
1 tsp dry mustard powder
300 g/10½ oz/1½ cups basmati rice
750 ml/1⅓ pints/3½ cups water
2 small leeks, trimmed and cut into 5
   mm/¼ inch slices

2 tbsp chopped fresh flat-leaf parsley
   or coriander (cilantro)
a squeeze of lemon juice
3–4 hard-boiled (hard-cooked) eggs,
   peeled and quartered
salt and pepper
lemon quarters, to serve

1 Put the fish in a frying pan (skillet) and pour in enough milk to just cover; add the bay leaves. Bring to the boil, then simmer gently, covered, for about 4 minutes. Remove from the heat and stand, covered, for about 10 minutes.

2 Using a slotted spoon, transfer the fish to a plate and cover loosely; set aside. Reserve the cooking milk, discarding the bay leaves.

3 Heat the oil and half the butter in a large pan over a medium heat. Add the onion and cook for about 2 minutes until soft. Stir in the curry powder and the mustard powder and cook for 1 minute.

4 Add the rice and stir for about 2 minutes until well coated. Add the water and bring to the boil; stir and reduce the heat to very low. Cook, covered, for 20–25 minutes until the rice is tender and the water absorbed.

5 Melt the remaining butter in a flameproof casserole, add the leeks and cook for about 4 minutes until soft. Fork the leeks into the hot rice. Add 2–3 tablespoons of the reserved milk to moisten.

6 Flake the fish off the skin into large pieces and fold into the rice. Stir in the parsley and lemon juice, then season with salt and pepper. Add a little more milk, if wished, then add the egg quarters. Serve, with lemon quarters.

Spanish Paella

This classic recipe gets its name from the wide metal pan traditionally used for cooking the dish – a paellera.

Serves 4

INGREDIENTS

120 ml/4 fl oz/½ cup olive oil
1.5 kg/3 lb 5 oz chicken, cut into
   8 pieces
350 g/12 oz chorizo sausage, cut into
   1 cm/½ inch pieces
115 g/4 oz cured ham, chopped
2 onions, finely chopped
2 red (bell) peppers, cored, deseeded
   and cut into 2.5 cm/1 inch pieces

4–6 garlic cloves
750 g/1 lb 10 oz/3¾ cups short-grain
   Spanish rice or Italian arborio rice
2 bay leaves
1 tsp dried thyme
1 tsp saffron threads, lightly crushed
225 ml/8 fl oz/1 cup dry white wine
1.5 litres/2¾ pints/6¼ cups chicken
   stock

115 g/4 oz fresh shelled or defrosted
   frozen peas
450 g/1 lb medium uncooked prawns
   (shrimp)
8 raw King prawns (shrimp), in shells
16 clams, very well scrubbed
16 mussels, very well scrubbed
salt and pepper
4 tbsp chopped fresh flat-leaf parsley

1 Heat half the oil in a 46 cm/ 18 inch paella pan or deep, wide frying pan (skillet) over a medium-high heat. Add the chicken and fry gently, turning, until golden brown. Remove from the pan and set aside.

2 Add the chorizo and ham to the pan and cook for about 7 minutes, stirring occasionally, until crisp. Remove and set aside.

3 Stir the onions into the pan and cook for about 3 minutes until soft. Add the (bell) peppers and garlic and cook until beginning to soften; remove and set aside.

4 Add the remaining oil to the pan and stir in the rice until well coated. Add the bay leaves, thyme and saffron and stir well. Pour in the wine, bubble, then pour in the stock, stirring well and scraping the bottom of the pan. Bring to the boil, stirring often.

5 Stir in the cooked vegetables. Add the chorizo, ham and chicken and gently bury in the rice. Reduce the heat and cook for 10 minutes, stirring occasionally.

6 Add the peas and prawns (shrimp) and cook for a further 5 minutes. Push the clams and mussels into the rice. Cover and cook over a very low heat for about 5 minutes until the rice is tender and the shellfish open. Discard any unopened clams or mussels. Season to taste.

7 Remove from heat, and stand, covered, for about 5 minutes. Sprinkle with parsley and serve.

Salmon Coulibiac

Coulibiac is probably the world's best fish pie. It was first made in the 19th century by French chefs working in the Imperial Russian courts.

Serves 6–8

INGREDIENTS

114 g/4 oz/8 tbsp butter, plus extra
   2 tbsp butter melted
2 onions, finely chopped
115 g/4 oz/generous ½ cup long-grain
   white rice
750 g/1 lb 10 oz skinned salmon fillet,
   poached in water, cooking liquid
   reserved

150 g/5½ oz mushrooms, thinly sliced
80 g/3 oz cooked spinach, chopped
2 tbsp chopped fresh dill
6 canned anchovy fillets in oil, drained
   and chopped
5 hard-boiled (hard-cooked) eggs,
   roughly chopped

grated rind and juice of 1 large lemon
375 g/12½ oz packet puff pastry
1 egg, beaten, for glaze
salt and pepper
lemon wedges and dill sprigs, to
   garnish

1 Melt half of the butter in a large saucepan, add half the onion and cook for about 2 minutes until soft. Stir in the rice for 2 minutes until well coated.

2 If necessary, add water to the reserved fish cooking liquid to make up to 225 ml/8 fl oz/1 cup. Add to the rice, bring to the boil, then cover and cook very gently for about 18 minutes. Allow to cool.

3 Melt the remaining butter in a frying pan (skillet), add the remaining onions and mushrooms and cook for about 8 minutes until there is no liquid. Add the spinach and dill. Season well, then cool.

4 Add the anchovies, eggs and lemon rind and juice to the mushroom mixture and toss well.

5 Roll out the puff pastry and cut into two squares, one 28 cm/11 inches square and the other 30 cm/12 inches square. Place the smaller piece on a lightly greased baking (cookie) sheet and spread half the mushroom mixture over, leaving a 2.5 cm/1 inch border; spoon over half the rice.

6 Centre the salmon on top of the rice layer and cover with the remaining rice. Spoon over the remaining mushroom mixture. Drizzle the melted butter over the top. Brush the pastry edges with egg, cover with the second square and seal the edges.

7 Brush with egg and mark a lattice pattern on top. Bake in a preheated oven 220°C/425°F/ Gas Mark 7 for about 35 minutes until golden. Rest on a wire rack , then serve garnished.

Stuffed Cabbage

Hailing from Eastern Europe, this recipe is a delicious way to stretch a small amount of meat.
Use the smaller cabbage leaves too – simply overlap them to create the size of the larger leaves.

Serves 6–8

INGREDIENTS

60 g/2 oz/1 cup fresh white
  breadcrumbs
120 ml/4 fl oz/½ cup milk
1 tbsp vegetable oil
1 onion, finely chopped
2 garlic cloves, finely chopped
450 g/1 lb minced (ground) beef steak
450 g/1 lb minced (ground) pork or veal
2 tbsp tomato ketchup (catsup)
3 tbsp chopped fresh dill

1 tsp chopped fresh thyme leaves
100 g/3½ oz/½ cup long-grain
  white rice
salt and pepper
1 large cabbage, such as Savoy, leaves
  separated and blanched

TOMATO SAUCE:
2 large onions, thinly sliced
2 tbsp olive oil

2 x 400 g/14 oz cans chopped
  tomatoes
450 ml/16 fl oz/2 cups sieved
  tomatoes or passata
50 ml/2 fl oz/¼ cup tomato ketchup
  (catsup)
grated rind and juice of 1 large lemon
2 tbsp light brown sugar
75 g/2¾ oz raisins

1 Combine the breadcrumbs and the milk; leave to soak. Cook the onion and garlic in the oil for about 2 minutes until soft, then set aside.

2 Place the beef and pork or veal in a bowl. Mix in the ketchup (catsup), herbs, rice and seasoning. Add the breadcrumbs, cooked onion and garlic.

3 To make the tomato sauce, cook the onions in the oil for 3 minutes until soft. Stir in the tomatoes and the remaining ingredients and bring to the boil, then simmer for about 15 minutes, stirring occasionally. Set aside.

4 To fill the leaves, spoon 1–2 tablespoons of the meat mixture on to a cabbage leaf above

the stem end. Fold the stem end over the filling, then fold over the sides. Roll up to enclose. Repeat with the remaining leaves.

5 Spoon enough tomato sauce to cover the base of a large baking dish. Arrange the filled cabbage rolls, seam-side down, in the dish. Spoon the remaining sauce over the rolls to just cover – add a little water if necessary. Cover tightly and bake in a preheated oven at 160°C/325°F/ Gas Mark 3 for about 1½ hours, basting once or twice.

6 Transfer the cabbage rolls to a serving plate and keep warm. Bubble the sauce to thicken, if necessary. Serve at once.

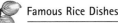

Mediterranean Stuffed Peppers

Serve the (bell) peppers with their tops for an attractive finish – blanch them with the peppers,
then bake separately for the last 10 minutes and place in position just before serving.

Serves 6

INGREDIENTS

6 large (bell) peppers, red, yellow and
   orange
200 g/7 oz/1 cup long-grain white rice
2–3 tbsp olive oil, plus extra for
   greasing and drizzling
1 large onion
2 stalks celery, chopped

2 garlic cloves, finely chopped
$^1/_2$ tsp ground cinnamon or allspice
75 g/2$^3/_4$ oz/$^1/_2$ cup raisins
4 tbsp pine kernels (nuts), lightly
   toasted
4 ripe plum tomatoes, deseeded and
   chopped

50 ml/2 fl oz/$^1/_4$ cup white wine
4 anchovy fillets, chopped
$^1/_2$ bunch chopped fresh parsley
$^1/_2$ bunch chopped fresh mint
6 tbsp freshly grated Parmesan cheese
salt and pepper
fresh tomato sauce, to serve (optional)

1 Using a sharp knife, slice off the tops of the (bell) peppers, then remove the cores and seeds. Blanch the (bell) peppers in boiling water for 2–3 minutes. Carefully remove and drain upside-down on a wire rack.

2 Bring a saucepan of salted water to the boil. Gradually pour in the rice and return to the boil; simmer until tender, but firm to the bite. Drain and rinse under cold running water. Set aside.

3 Heat the oil in a large frying pan (skillet). Add the onion and celery and cook for 2 minutes. Stir in the garlic, cinnamon and raisins and cook for 1 minute. Fork in the rice, then stir in the pine kernels (nuts), tomatoes, wine, anchovies, parsley and mint and cook for 4 minutes. Remove from the heat, add salt and pepper and stir in half the Parmesan.

4 Brush the bottom of a baking dish with a little oil. Divide the rice mixture equally among the peppers. Arrange in the dish and sprinkle with the remaining Parmesan. Drizzle with a little more oil and pour in enough water to come 1 cm/$^1/_2$ inch up the sides of the peppers. Loosely cover the dish with kitchen foil.

5 Bake in a preheated oven at 180°C/350°F/Gas Mark 4 for about 40 minutes. Uncover and cook for a further 10 minutes. Serve hot with tomato sauce.

Jamaican Rice and Peas

A favourite Caribbean dish, this was probably originally made with 'pigeon peas', but you can use any dried bean you like. The spicy salsa is a modern twist to this all-in-one dish.

Serves 6–8

INGREDIENTS

450 g/1 lb/2 cups dried beans, such as black-eyed beans, black beans or small red kidney beans, soaked in cold water overnight
2 tbsp vegetable oil
1 large onion, chopped
2–3 garlic cloves, finely chopped
2 red chillies, deseeded and chopped
450 g/1 lb/2¼ cups long-grain white rice

400 ml/14 fl oz/⅔ cup canned coconut milk
¾ tsp dried thyme
salt

TOMATO SALSA:
4 ripe tomatoes, deseeded and cut into 5 mm/¼ inch dice
1 red onion, finely chopped

4 tbsp chopped fresh coriander (cilantro)
2 garlic cloves, finely chopped
1–2 jalapeño chillies, or to taste, deseeded and thinly sliced
1–2 tbsp extra-virgin olive oil
1 tbsp fresh lime juice
1 tsp light brown sugar
salt and pepper

1 Drain the soaked beans, rinse and put in a large pan. Cover with cold water by about 5 cm/2 inches and bring to the boil, over a high heat, skimming off any foam.

2 Boil the beans for about 10 minutes (to remove any toxins), drain and rinse again. Return to the pan, cover with cold water again and bring to the boil over a high heat.

3 Reduce the heat and keep at a moderate simmer, partially covered, for about 1¼–1½ hours for black-eyed beans, 1½–2 hours for black beans or 50–60 minutes for kidney beans, until tender. Drain reserving the cooking liquid.

4 Heat the oil in another pan. Add the onion and cook for about 2 minutes until soft. Stir in the garlic and chillies and cook for

a further minute. Add the rice and stir until well coated.

5 Stir in the coconut milk, thyme and about 1 teaspoon salt. Add the cooked beans and 450 ml/16 fl oz/2 cups of the reserved bean cooking liquid to cover; add more bean liquid if necessary. Bring the mixture to the boil, then reduce the heat to low, cover tightly and cook for 20–25 minutes.

6 Meanwhile, make the tomato salsa: combine all the ingredients in a bowl and stand, loosely covered, at room temperature.

7 Remove the rice from the heat and stand, covered, for 5 minutes, then fork into a serving bowl. Serve hot with the salsa.

Creole Jambalaya

A rich, rice-based stew, combining a fabulous mix of meat and seafood with exciting peppery flavourings, Jambalaya captures the true essence of Creole cooking.

Serves 6–8

INGREDIENTS

2 tbsp vegetable oil

80 g/3 oz piece good-quality smoked ham, cut into bite-sized pieces

80 g/3 oz/$^1/_2$ cup andouille or pure smoked pork sausage, such as Polish kielbasa, cut into chunks

2 large onions, finely chopped

3–4 stalks celery, finely chopped

2 green (bell) peppers, cored, deseeded and finely chopped

2 garlic cloves, finely chopped

225 g/8 oz boned chicken breast or thighs, skinned and cut into pieces

4 ripe tomatoes, skinned and chopped

175 ml/6 fl oz/$^3/_4$ cup passata or sieved strained tomatoes

450 ml/16 fl oz/2 cups fish stock

400 g/14 oz/2 cups long-grain white rice

4 spring onions (scallions), cut into 2.5 cm/1 inch pieces

250 g/9 oz peeled raw prawns (shrimp), tails on, if wished

250 g/9 oz cooked white crab meat

12 oysters, shelled (shucked), with their liquor

SEASONING MIX:

2 dried bay leaves

1 tsp salt

1$^1/_2$–2 tsp cayenne pepper, or to taste

1$^1/_2$ tsp dried oregano

1 tsp ground white pepper, or to taste

1 tsp black pepper, or to taste

1 To make the seasoning mix, mix the ingredients in a bowl.

2 Heat the oil in a flameproof casserole over a medium heat. Add the smoked ham and the sausage and cook for about 8 minutes, stirring frequently, until golden. Using a slotted spoon, transfer to a large plate.

3 Add the onions, celery and (bell) peppers to the casserole and cook for about 4 minutes until just softened. Stir in the garlic, then remove and set aside.

4 Add the chicken pieces to the casserole and cook for 3–4 minutes until beginning to colour. Stir in the seasoning mix to coat.

5 Return the ham, sausage and vegetables to the casserole and stir to combine. Add the chopped tomatoes and passata, then pour in the stock. Bring to the boil.

6 Stir in the rice and reduce the heat to a simmer. Cook for about 12 minutes. Uncover, stir in the spring onions (scallions) and prawns (shrimp) and cook, covered, for 4 minutes.

7 Add the crab meat and oysters with their liquor and gently stir in. Cook until the rice is just tender, and the oysters slightly firm. Remove from the heat and leave to stand, covered, for about 3 minutes before serving.

Murgh Pullau

This delicately flavoured dish is from North India. Traditionally the meat and rice are cooked together for ease of preparation, but here they are cooked separately to ensure perfect timing.

Serves 4–6

INGREDIENTS

350 g/12 oz/1¾ cups basmati rice
60 g/2 oz/4 tbsp ghee or butter
115 g/4 oz/1 cup flaked (slivered) almonds
80 g/3 oz/¾ cup unsalted, shelled pistachio nuts
4–6 boned chicken breasts, skinned and each cut into 4 pieces

2 onions, thinly sliced
2 garlic cloves, chopped finely
2.5 cm/1 inch piece fresh ginger root, peeled and chopped
6 green cardamom pods, lightly crushed
4–6 whole cloves
2 bay leaves
1 tsp ground coriander

½ tsp cayenne pepper
225 ml/8 fl oz/1 cup natural yogurt
225 ml/8 fl oz/1 cup double (heavy) cream
2–4 tbsp chopped fresh coriander (cilantro) or mint
225 g/8 oz seedless green grapes, halved if large

1 Bring a saucepan of salted water to the boil. Gradually pour in the rice, return to the boil, then simmer until the rice is just tender. Drain and rinse under cold running water; set aside.

2 Heat the ghee in a deep frying pan (skillet) over a medium-high heat. Add the almonds and pistachios and cook for 3 minutes, stirring, until light golden. Remove and reserve.

3 Add the chicken to the pan and cook for about 5 minutes, turning, until golden. Remove and reserve. Add the onions to the pan. Cook for about 10 minutes until golden. Stir in the garlic and spices and cook for 3 minutes.

4 Add 2–3 tablespoons of the yogurt and cook, stirring, until all the moisture evaporates. Continue adding the rest of the yogurt in the same way.

5 Return the chicken and nuts to the pan and stir to coat. Stir in 120 ml/4 fl oz/½ cup boiling water. Season with salt and pepper and cook, covered, over a low heat for about 10 minutes until the chicken is cooked through. Stir in the cream, coriander (cilantro) and grapes and remove from the heat.

6 Fork the rice into a bowl, then gently fold in the chicken and sauce. Stand for 5 minutes. Serve.

Mumbar

This Middle Eastern dish is basically a long sausage coiled into a frying pan (skillet) to simmer.
The baharat, or spice mix, is typical of much of the cooking in the Gulf, as is basmati rice and onions.

Serves 6–8

INGREDIENTS

100 g/3$\frac{1}{2}$ oz/$\frac{1}{2}$ cup basmati rice
900 g/2 lb finely minced (ground) lamb
1 small onion, finely chopped
3–4 garlic cloves, crushed
1 bunch each flat-leaf parsley and
    coriander (cilantro) finely chopped
2–3 tbsp tomato ketchup (catsup)

1 tbsp vegetable oil
pared rind and juice of 1 lime
700 ml /1$\frac{1}{4}$ pints/3 cups hot lamb stock
salt and pepper

BAHARAT SEASONING MIX:
2 tbsp black peppercorns

1 tbsp coriander (cilantro) seeds
2 tsp whole cloves
1$\frac{1}{2}$ tsp cumin seeds
1 tsp cardamom seeds
1 cinnamon stick, broken into small pieces
1 whole nutmeg
2 tbsp hot paprika

1 To make the baharat, grind the first 6 ingredients into a fine powder. Grate the whole nutmeg into the mix and stir in the paprika. Store in an airtight jar.

2 Bring a pan of salted water to the boil. Pour in the rice, return to the boil, then simmer until the rice is tender, but firm to the bite. Drain and rinse.

3 Place the lamb in a large bowl and break up with a fork. Add the onion, garlic, parsley, coriander (cilantro), ketchup (catsup) and 1 teaspoon of the baharat. Stir in the cooked rice and season. Squeeze the mixture to make it paste-like.

4 Divide into 4-6 pieces and roll each into a sausage of 2.5cm/1 inch thick. Brush a 23–25 cm/9–10 inch frying pan (skillet) with the oil. Starting in the centre of the pan, coil the sausage pieces, joining each piece, to form one long coiled sausage.

5 Press lightly to make an even layer, then tuck the lime rind between the spaces of the sausage. Add the lime juice to the pan. Pour in the hot stock and cover with a heatproof plate to keep in place.

6 Bring to the boil, then simmer gently for about 10 minutes. Cover; continue to cook for 15 minutes. Remove from the heat, drain and slide the sausage on to a serving plate. Sprinkle with a little more of the baharat to serve.

Lamb Biriyani

For an authentic finishing touch, garnish with crisply-fried onion rings,
toasted slivered almonds, chopped pistachio nuts and pieces of edible silver foil (vark).

Serves 6–8

INGREDIENTS

900 g/2 lb boned lean leg or shoulder of lamb, cut into 2.5 cm/1 inch cubes
6 garlic cloves, finely chopped
4 cm/1½ inch piece fresh ginger root, peeled and finely chopped
1 tbsp ground cinnamon
1 tbsp green cardamom pods, crushed to expose the black seeds
1 tsp whole cloves
2 tsp coriander seeds, crushed

2 tsp cumin seeds, crushed
½ tsp ground turmeric (optional)
2 fresh green chillies, deseeded and chopped
grated rind and juice of 1 lime
1 bunch fresh coriander (cilantro), chopped finely
1 bunch fresh mint, chopped finely
120 ml/4 fl oz/½ cup natural yogurt
115 g/4 oz/8 tbsp ghee, butter or vegetable oil

4 onions, 3 thinly sliced and 1 finely chopped
600 g/1 lb 5 oz/3 cups basmati rice
2 cinnamon sticks, broken
½ a whole nutmeg, freshly grated
3–4 tbsp raisins
1.2 litres/2 pints/5 cups chicken stock or water
225 ml/8 fl oz/1 cup hot milk
1 tsp saffron threads, slightly crushed
salt and pepper

1 Combine the lamb with the garlic, ginger, cinnamon, cardamom, cloves, coriander and cumin seeds, turmeric, chillies, lime rind and juice, 2 tablespoons each of coriander and mint and yogurt. Marinate for 2–3 hours.

2 Heat about half the fat in a large frying pan (skillet), add

the sliced onions and cook for about 8 minutes until lightly browned. Add the meat and any juices; season with salt and pepper. Stir in about 225 ml/8 fl oz/1 cup water and simmer for 18–20 minutes until the lamb is just cooked.

3 Meanwhile, heat the fat left over in a flameproof casserole.

Add the chopped onion and cook for 2 minutes until soft. Add the rice and cook, stirring, for 3–4 minutes until well coated. Add the cinnamon, nutmeg, raisins and stock. Bring to the boil, stirring once or twice, and season with salt and pepper. Simmer, covered, over a low heat for 12 minutes until the liquid is reduced but the rice is still a little firm.

4 Pour the hot milk over the saffron; stand for 10 minutes. Remove the rice from the heat and stir in the saffron-milk. Fold in the lamb mixture. Cover and bake in a preheated oven at 350°C/180°F/ Gas Mark 4 until the rice is cooked and the liquid absorbed.

Red Pork Curry with Jasmine-scented Rice

Thai food has become so popular in recent years that most ingredients can be found in your local supermarket. Using a food processor may not be authentic, but it saves time and energy.

Serves 4–6

INGREDIENTS

900 g/2 lb boned pork shoulder, cut into thin slices
700 ml/1¼ pints/3 cups coconut milk
2 fresh red chillies, deseeded and thinly sliced
2 tbsp Thai fish sauce
2 tsp brown sugar
1 large red (bell) pepper, cored, deseeded and thinly sliced
6 kaffir lime leaves, shredded
½ bunch fresh mint leaves, shredded

½ bunch Thai basil leaves or Italian-style basil, shredded
jasmine-scented or Thai fragrant rice, cooked according to the packet instructions and kept warm

RED CURRY PASTE:
1 tbsp coriander (cilantro) seeds
2 tsp cumin seeds
2 tsp black or white peppercorns
1 tsp salt, or to taste

5–8 dried hot red chillies
3–4 shallots, chopped
6–8 garlic cloves
5 cm/2 inch piece fresh galangal or ginger root, peeled and coarsely chopped
2 tsp kaffir lime rind or 2 fresh lime leaves, chopped
1 tbsp ground red chilli powder
1 tbsp shrimp paste
2 stalks lemon grass, thinly sliced

1 To make the red curry paste, grind the coriander seeds, cumin seeds, peppercorns and salt to a fine powder. Add the chillies, one by one, according to taste, until ground.

2 Put the shallots, garlic, galangal or ginger root, kaffir lime rind, chilli powder and

shrimp paste in a food processor. Process for about 1 minute. Add the ground spices and process again. Adding water, a few drops at a time, continue to process until a thick paste forms. Scrape into a bowl and stir in the lemon grass.

3 Put about half the red curry paste in a large deep heavy-

based frying pan (skillet) with the pork. Cook over a medium heat for 2–3 minutes, stirring gently, until the pork is evenly coated and begins to brown.

4 Stir in the coconut milk and bring to the boil. Cook, stirring frequently, for about 10 minutes. Reduce the heat, stir in the chillies, Thai fish sauce and brown sugar and simmer for about 20 minutes. Add the red (bell) pepper and simmer for a further 10 minutes.

5 Add the lime leaves and half the mint and basil to the curry. Transfer to a serving dish, sprinkle with the remaining mint and basil and serve with the rice.

Mee Krob

Everyone loves the spiciness and crunch of this traditional Thai noodle dish.
Fry the rice noodles little by little to avoid too much spattering and smoke during cooking.

Serves 4–6

INGREDIENTS

vegetable oil, for frying
350 g/12 oz fine rice vermicelli
    noodles, unsoaked
4 eggs, lightly beaten
80 g/3 oz boned lean leg of pork, thinly
    sliced

80 g/3 oz boned chicken breast,
    skinned and thinly sliced
80 g/3 oz small peeled prawns (shrimp)
4–6 spring onions (scallions), thinly
    sliced on the diagonal
3–4 fresh red chillies, thinly sliced on
    the diagonal

4 tbsp rice vinegar
4 tbsp light soy sauce
4 tbsp Thai fish sauce
4–6 tbsp chicken stock or water
4 tbsp sugar
1 tsp coriander seeds, lightly crushed
4 tbsp chopped fresh coriander (cilantro)

1 Heat at least 7.5 cm/3 inches of vegetable oil in a deep-fat fryer or wok to 180–190°C/350–375°F or until a cube of bread browns in 30 seconds.

2 Gently separate the layers of noodles, then carefully fry, one layer at a time, for 10–15 seconds until golden. Transfer to paper towels to drain; set aside.

3 Heat 1–2 tablespoons of the hot oil in a large non-stick frying pan (skillet). Pour in the beaten egg to form a thin layer and cook for about 1 minute until just set. Turn and cook for 5 seconds longer. Slide out of the pan and cool slightly. Cut in half and roll up each half, then slice into 5mm/¼ inch strips. Set aside.

4 Heat 2 more tablespoons of the oil in a wok or large, deep frying pan (skillet) over a medium-high heat. Add the pork and chicken slices and stir-fry for about 2 minutes, or until cooked.

5 Add the prawns (shrimp), spring onions (scallions) and chillies and stir to mix. Push the meat and vegetables to one side. Add the vinegar, soy sauce, fish sauce, sugar and coriander seeds to the space in the pan, bubble gently, then stir into the meat mixture. Stir in the omelette and half the fresh coriander (cilantro).

6 Add the warm noodles, turn gently and sprinkle with the remaining coriander (cilantro).

Nasi Goreng

A meal in itself, this mouthwatering fried rice dish is bursting with the exotic flavours of Indonesia. The perfect supper dish!

Serves 4

INGREDIENTS

1 large onion, chopped
2–3 garlic cloves
1 tsp shrimp paste
2 red chillies, deseeded and chopped
vegetable oil
3 eggs, lightly beaten
450 g/1 lb beef rump steak, about
    1 cm/½ inch thick
2 carrots, cut into thin matchsticks

175 g/6 oz Chinese long beans
    or green beans, cut into 2.5 cm/
    1 inch pieces
6 small spring onions (scallions),
    cut into 1 cm/½ inch pieces
250 g/9 oz raw shelled prawns
    (shrimp)
750 g/1 lb 10 oz/3¾ cups cooked
    long-grain white rice, at room
    temperature

6 tbsp dark soy sauce

TO GARNISH:
4 tbsp ready-fried onion flakes
10 cm/4 inch piece cucumber,
    deseeded and cut into thin sticks
2 tbsp chopped fresh coriander
    (cilantro)

1 Put the onion, garlic, shrimp paste and chillies into a food processor and process until a paste forms. Add a little oil and process until smooth. Set aside.

2 Heat 1–2 tablespoons oil in a large, non-stick frying pan (skillet). Pour in the egg to form a thin layer and cook for 1 minute until just set. Turn and cook for 5 seconds on the other side. Slide out and cut in half. Roll up each half, then slice into 5 mm/¼ inch wide strips. Set aside.

3 Heat 2 tablespoons oil in the same pan over a high heat and add the steak. Cook for 2 minutes on each side to brown and seal, but do not cook completely. Cool, then cut into thin strips and reserve.

4 Heat 2 tablespoons oil in a large wok over a medium-high heat. Add the reserved chilli paste and cook, stirring frequently, for about 3 minutes. Add 2 tablespoons of oil, the carrots and long beans. Stir-fry for about 2 minutes. Add the spring onions (scallions), prawns (shrimp) and the beef strips and stir-fry until the prawns are pink.

5 Stir in the rice, half the sliced omelette, 2 tablespoons soy sauce and 50 ml/2 fl oz/¼ cup water. Cover and steam for 1 minute. Spoon into a serving dish, top with the remaining omelette and drizzle with the remaining soy sauce. Sprinkle with a selection of the garnishes and serve.

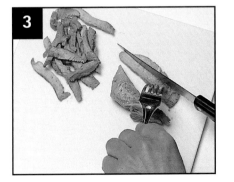

Iranian Steamed Crusty Rice

The trick is to achieve a light fragrant rice with a crunchy golden brown crust;
it may take several attempts, but it's worth the effort!

Serves 6

INGREDIENTS

425 g/15 oz/2 cups plus 1 tbsp basmati or long-grain white rice	salt 60 g/2 oz/4 tbsp butter or ghee	50 ml/2 fl oz/¼ cup water

1. Bring at least 2 litres/3½ pints/8 cups of water to the boil. Add 2 tablespoons of salt. Gradually add the rice, then simmer for 7–10 minutes until almost tender; stir gently occasionally. Drain and rinse under warm running water to remove any starch.

2. Heat the butter or ghee with the water in a large heavy-based saucepan over a medium-high heat until the butter melts and the water is steaming; remove half of this mixture and reserve. Spoon enough rice into the pan to cover the bottom, smoothing lightly and evenly.

3. Spoon the remaining rice into the pan. Cover the rice with a thin tea towel (dish cloth), then cover the pan tightly and reduce the heat to very low. Cook for 15 minutes.

4. Remove the covers and, with the handle of a wooden spoon, gently poke several holes into the rice to allow the steam to escape.

5. Pour the remaining butter-water mixture over the rice, re-cover as before and cook for 10–15 minutes. Uncover and transfer the pan to a chilled surface (see Cook's Tip); this helps to loosen the crust from the bottom.

6. Using a fork, fluff the loose rice into a serving bowl. Break up the crusty brown layer into pieces and arrange around the serving dish. Traditionally, the honoured guest got the crusty layer!

COOK'S TIP

To chill the work surface for cooling down the saucepan of hot rice, place 2 ice-cube trays on the work surface ahead of time.

Chinese Fried Rice

This simple Cantonese recipe for using leftover rice has become a world-wide speciality in Chinese restaurants. Enjoy this homemade version, which includes ham and prawns (shrimp).

Serves 4–6

INGREDIENTS

2–3 tbsp groundnut or vegetable oil

2 onions, halved and cut lengthways into thin wedges

2 garlic cloves, thinly sliced

2.5 cm/1 inch piece fresh ginger root, peeled, sliced and cut into slivers

200 g/7 oz cooked ham, thinly sliced

750 g/1 lb 10 oz/4 cups cooked, cold long-grain white rice

250 g/9 oz cooked peeled prawns (shrimp)

115 g/4 oz canned water chestnuts, sliced

3 eggs

3 tsp sesame oil

4–6 spring onions (scallions), diagonally sliced into 2.5 cm/1 inch pieces

2 tbsp dark soy sauce or Thai fish sauce

1 tbsp sweet chilli sauce

2 tbsp chopped fresh coriander (cilantro) or flat-leaf parsley

salt and pepper

1 Heat 2–3 tablespoons groundnut oil in a wok or large, deep frying pan (skillet) until very hot. Add the onions and stir-fry for about 2 minutes until beginning to soften. Add the garlic and ginger and stir-fry for another minute. Add the ham strips and stir to combine.

2 Add the cold cooked rice and stir to mix with the vegetables and ham. Stir in the prawns (shrimp) and the water chestnuts. Stir in 2 tablespoons water and cover the pan quickly. Continue to cook for 2 minutes, shaking the pan occasionally to prevent sticking and to allow the rice to heat through.

3 Beat the eggs with 1 teaspoon of the sesame oil and season with salt and pepper. Make a well in the centre of the rice mixture, add the eggs and immediately stir, gradually drawing the rice into the eggs.

4 Stir in the spring onions (scallions), soy sauce and chilli sauce and stir-fry; stir in a little more water if the rice looks dry or is sticking. Drizzle in the remaining sesame oil and stir. Season to taste with salt and pepper.

5 Remove from the heat, wipe the edge of the wok or frying pan (skillet) and sprinkle with the coriander (cilantro). Serve immediately from the pan.

Malayan Rice Noodle Soup

This meal-in-a-bowl soup is based on a dish called
Laska in Malayan and has a very authentic flavour.

Serves 4–6

INGREDIENTS

1.25 kg/2 lb 12 oz corn-fed or
  free-range chicken
1 tsp black peppercorns
2 tbsp groundnut or vegetable oil
2 onions, thinly sliced
2–3 garlic cloves, minced
5 cm/1 inch piece fresh ginger root,
  peeled and thinly sliced
1 tsp ground coriander (cilantro)

2 fresh red chillies, deseeded and
  thinly sliced on the diagonal
1/2–1 tsp ground turmeric
1–2 tsp Madras curry paste
400 ml/14 fl oz/1 2/3 cups canned
  coconut milk
450 g/1 lb large raw prawns (shrimp),
  peeled and deveined

1/2 small head of Chinese leaves, thinly
  shredded
1 tsp sugar
2 spring onions (scallions), thinly sliced
115 g/4 oz bean-sprouts
250 g/9 oz rice noodles, rice vermicelli
  or rice sticks, soaked according to
  packet instructions
handful of fresh mint leaves, to garnish

1 To make the stock, put the chicken in a large saucepan with the peppercorns and enough cold water just to cover. Bring to the boil, then simmer for 1 hour, skimming off any foam.

2 Remove the chicken; cool. Skim any fat from the liquid and strain through muslin; set aside. Remove the chicken meat from the carcass and shred.

3 Heat the oil in a deep frying pan (skillet) until very hot. Add the onions to the pan and stir-fry for about 2 minutes until they begin to colour. Stir in the garlic, ginger, coriander (cilantro), chillies, turmeric and curry paste. Transfer to a large pan and slowly stir in the stock. Simmer, partially covered, over low heat for about 20 minutes or until the stock has slightly reduced.

4 Add the coconut milk, prawns (shrimp) and Chinese leaves to the simmering stock, cook for about 3 minutes, stirring occasionally, until the prawns (shrimp) are pink. Add the shredded chicken and cook for a further 2 minutes.

5 Drain the noodles and divide between 4–6 bowls. Ladle the hot stock and vegetables over the noodles. Make sure each serving has some of the prawns and the shredded chicken. Garnish with mint leaves and serve immediately.

COOK'S TIP

Corn-fed chickens are reared on a
diet of sweetcorn, which gives them
a distinctive yellow colour and
delicious flavour.

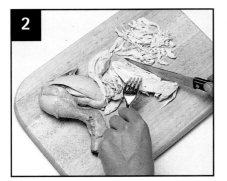

Singapore Noodles

Although called Singapore noodles this spicy rice noodle dish probably evolved in Hong Kong,
where the diverse cultures of South-East Asia often come together.

Serves 4–6

INGREDIENTS

60 g/2 oz dried Chinese mushrooms
225 g/8 oz rice vermicelli noodles
2–3 tbsp groundnut or vegetable oil
6–8 garlic cloves, thinly sliced
2–3 shallots, thinly sliced
2.5 cm/1 inch piece fresh ginger root,
  peeled and thinly sliced
4–5 fresh red chillies, deseeded and
  thinly sliced on the diagonal
225 g/8 oz boned chicken breasts,
  skinned and thinly sliced

225 g/8 oz mangetout (snow peas),
  thinly sliced on the diagonal
225 g/8 oz Chinese leaves, thinly
  shredded
225 g/8 oz cooked peeled prawns
  (shrimp)
6–8 water chestnuts, sliced
2 spring onions (scallions), thinly
  sliced on the diagonal
2 tbsp chopped fresh coriander
  (cilantro) or mint

SINGAPORE CURRY SAUCE:
2 tbsp rice wine or dry sherry
2 tbsp soy sauce
3 tbsp medium or hot Madras curry
  powder
1 tbsp sugar
400 ml/14 fl oz/1^2/$_3$ cups canned
  coconut milk
1 tsp salt
4–5 grinds black pepper

1 To make the curry sauce, whisk the rice wine and soy sauce into the curry powder, then stir in the remaining ingredients.

2 Put the Chinese mushrooms in a small bowl and add enough boiling water to cover. Leave for about 15 minutes until softened. Lift out and squeeze out the liquid. Discard any stems, then slice thinly and set aside. Soak the rice noodles according to the instructions on the packet, then drain well.

3 Heat the oil in a wok or deep frying pan (skillet) over a medium-high heat. Add the garlic, shallots, ginger and chillies and stir-fry for about 30 seconds. Add the chicken and mangetout (snow peas) and stir-fry for about 2 minutes. Add the Chinese leaves, prawns (shrimp), water chestnuts, mushrooms and spring onions (scallions) and stir-fry for 1–2 minutes. Add the curry sauce and noodles; stir-fry for 5 minutes. Add the coriander (cilantro); serve.

Vietnamese Spring Rolls

Vietnamese spring rolls use a very thin rice paper as a wrapper which gives them their characteristic thin, crispy texture.

Makes 25–30 rolls

INGREDIENTS

25–30 rice paper wrappers
4–5 tbsp plain (all-purpose) flour, mixed
  to a paste with 4–5 tbsp water
vegetable oil, for frying
sliced spring onions (scallions), to
  garnish

FILLING:
15 g/½ oz dried Chinese mushrooms
1–2 tbsp groundnut or vegetable oil

1 small onion, finely chopped
3–4 garlic cloves
4 cm/1½ inch piece fresh ginger root,
  peeled and chopped
225 g/8 oz minced (ground) pork
2 spring onions (scallions), finely
  chopped
115 g/4 oz fresh bean-sprouts
4 water chestnuts, chopped
2 tbsp fresh chives, thinly sliced

175 g/6 oz small cooked peeled prawns
  (shrimp), coarsely chopped
1 tsp oyster sauce
1 tsp light soy sauce
60 g/2 oz rice vermicelli or cellophane
  noodles, soaked according to packet
  instructions
salt and pepper

1 To make the filling, cover the Chinese mushrooms with boiling water. Stand for about 15 minutes until softened. and squeeze out the liquid. Discard any stems and slice thinly.

2 Heat the oil in a wok over high heat. Add the onion, garlic and ginger and stir-fry for 2 minutes. Add the pork and soaked mushrooms and stir-fry for about 4 minutes until the pork is cooked and any liquid evaporates. Stir in the spring onions (scallions). Transfer to a bowl; cool.

3 Stir in the bean-sprouts, water chestnuts, chives and prawns (shrimp) with the oyster and soy sauces. Season with salt and pepper. Add the noodles and toss.

4 To assemble the spring rolls, soften a rice paper wrapper in warm water for a few seconds, then drain on a clean dry tea towel (dish cloth). Put 2 tablespoons of the filling near one edge of the wrapper, fold the edge over the filling to cover, then fold in each side and roll up. Seal with a little of the flour paste; set aside. Make the remaining rolls.

5 Heat about 10 cm/4 inches of oil in a deep-fat fryer to 180–190°C/350–375°F or until a cube of bread browns in 30 seconds. Fry the spring rolls a few at a time for about 2 minutes, turning once or twice, until golden. Drain on paper towels, then serve garnished with spring onion (scallions).

Japanese Sushi

These little snacks are made with special seasoned rice and a variety of toppings. Mix any remaining rice with the salmon trimmings and roll in toasted sesame seeds.

Serves 4–6

INGREDIENTS

400 g/14 oz/2 cups sushi rice
4 tbsp Japanese rice vinegar
1½ tbsp caster (superfine) sugar
1½ tsp salt
1½ tbsp mirin (Japanese rice wine)

NORIMAKI SUSHI:
2 eggs
pinch of turmeric
1–2 tbsp vegetable oil

4 sheets dried nori seaweed
115 g/4 oz smoked salmon slices, cut
   into 7.5 cm/3 inch pieces
½ cucumber, lightly peeled, quartered,
   deseeded, then thinly sliced lengthways
fresh chives

NIGIRI SUSHI:
16 cooked peeled prawns (shrimp)
wasabi paste (Japanese horseradish)
80 g/3 oz smoked salmon fillet, cut
   into 5 mm/¼ inch slices
sesame seeds, lightly toasted

TO SERVE:
pickled ginger
Japanese soy sauce

1 Bring 540 ml/17 fl oz/2⅛ cups water and the rice to the boil, then simmer, covered, for 20 minutes until just tender. Stand for 10 minutes, covered.

2 Bring to the boil the vinegar, sugar, salt and mirin. Pour the vinegar mixture evenly over the surface of the rice. Quickly blend into the rice, fanning the rice at the same time as it cools.

3 For the norimaki sushi, beat the eggs with the turmeric and 1 teaspoon of the oil, then use to make 2 omelettes, cooking in the remaining oil. Cut in half.

4 Pass the sheets of nori over a flame for a few minutes to toast. Lay a piece of nori, toasted-side down, on a bamboo sushi mat. Lay an omelette half on top, leaving a border around the edge.

Spread a thin layer of sushi rice over. Place a piece of smoked salmon on the bottom third of the rice, trimming to fit, and top with cucumber slices and a few chives.

5 Moisten the border of the nori with a little water and, using the mat as a guide, roll up. Repeat with the rest and leave to set, seam-side down. Cut into 2.5 cm/1 inch slices, cover and chill.

6 For the nigiri sushi, using wet hands, shape 2 tablespoons of the rice at a time into oblongs or ovals. Top with 2 prawns, or a dab of wasabi and some smoked salmon. Sprinkle with the toasted sesame seeds. Serve the sushi with the pickled ginger and Japanese soy sauce.

Puddings, & Cakes Pastries

One of the best ways to use rice is in desserts. Its delicate flavour and starchy characteristics are ideal for many puddings, cakes and sweets. Who can resist Meringue-Topped Rice Pudding, a thick creamy vanilla-scented rice topped with a sweet golden meringue – the perfect dessert for a cold winter night?

Every nationality seems to have developed a rice pudding, from the grand moulded Riz à l'Impératrice of France, to the classic Indian rice pudding, Kesari Kheer, which is tinted a stunning yellow with saffron. Sometimes only ground rice or rice flour is cooked with milk until it thickens into a rich creamy dish, like the Lebanese Almond Rice Pudding – absolutely delicious.

Rice gives texture to cakes like the Italian Lemon Rice Cake, a divine creation flavoured with rum and dried fruit, and the Rice Muffins, delicious with amaretti butter. An Italian ice cream is given an interesting twist with the addition of rice, while Spicy Carrot-rice Cake is a variation on an old favourite. Rice flour replaces a little flour in baked goods like Scottish Shortbread and Persian Rice Cookies, where it lends a fine texture and delicate flavour.

Meringue-topped Rice Pudding

Probably Scandinavian in origin, this mouthwatering pudding is thickened with cornflour (cornstarch) and egg yolks, making it extra rich and comforting.

Serves 6–8

INGREDIENTS

120 ml/4 fl oz/^{1}/$_2$ cup water
1.2 litres/2 pints/5 cups milk
100 g/3^1/$_2$ oz/^{1}/$_2$ cup long-grain white
   rice
2–3 strips of lemon rind

1 cinnamon stick
1 vanilla pod, split
115 g/4 oz/^{2}/$_3$ cup sugar
3 tbsp cornflour (cornstarch)
4 egg yolks

MERINGUE:
6 egg whites
^{1}/$_4$ tsp cream of tartar
225 g/8 oz/1 cup plus 2 tbsp caster
   (superfine) sugar

1 Bring the water and 225 ml/ 8 fl oz/1 cup of the milk to the boil in a large heavy-based saucepan. Add the rice, lemon rind, cinnamon stick and vanilla pod and reduce the heat to low. Cover and simmer for about 20 minutes until the rice is tender and all the liquid is absorbed. Remove the lemon rind, cinnamon stick and vanilla pod and add the remaining milk; return to the boil.

2 Stir together the sugar and the cornflour (cornstarch). Stir in a little of the hot rice-milk to make

a paste, then stir into the pan of rice. Cook, stirring constantly, until the mixture boils and thickens. Boil for 1 minute, then remove from the heat to cool slightly.

3 Beat the egg yolks until smooth. Stir a large spoonful of the hot rice mixture into the yolks, beating until well blended, then stir into the rice mixture. Pour into a 3 litre/5¼ pint/12 cup baking dish.

4 To make the meringue, beat the egg whites with the cream of tartar in a large bowl to form stiff

peaks. Add the sugar, 2 tablespoons at a time, beating well after each addition, until stiff and glossy.

5 Gently spoon the meringue over the top of the rice pudding, spreading evenly. Make swirls with the back of the spoon.

6 Bake in a preheated oven at 150°C/300°F/Gas Mark 2 for about 1 hour until the top is golden and set. Turn off the oven, open the door and allow the pudding to cool in the oven. Serve warm, at room temperature, or cold.

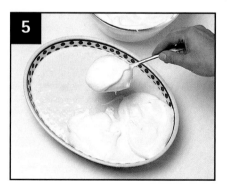

Basmati Pudding with Bay & Orange

This homely yet sophisticated rice pudding is surprisingly easy to make; the bay and orange are a delicious combination.

Serves 4

INGREDIENTS

600 ml/1 pint/2½ cups milk
225 m/8 fl oz/1 cup single (light) cream
4 fresh bay leaves, washed and gently bruised

50 g/2 oz/4 tbsp basmati or long-grain white rice
60 g/2 oz/¼ cup sugar
2 tbsp sultanas (golden raisins) or raisins

grated rind of 1 orange
1 tsp vanilla essence (extract)
2 tbsp pine kernels (nuts) or green pistachios
fancy biscuits (cookies), to serve

1 Put the milk and cream in a medium heavy-based saucepan and bring to the boil over a medium heat, stirring occasionally to prevent sticking.

2 Add the bay leaves, then sprinkle in the rice. Reduce the heat to low and simmer gently for about 1 hour, stirring occasionally, until the rice is tender and the mixture is thickened and creamy.

3 Stir in the sugar, sultanas (golden raisins) and orange rind and stir frequently until the sugar is dissolved and the fruit is plump. Remove from the heat, discard the bay leaves and stir in the vanilla.

4 Meanwhile, toast the pine kernels (nuts) in a small frying pan (skillet) until golden.

5 Spoon the pudding into individual bowls and sprinkle with the toasted nuts. Serve warm, or refrigerate to thicken and chill. Handle the biscuits separately.

VARIATION

Bay has a lovely flavour and goes well with rice, but, if preferred, you can substitute a cinnamon stick, lightly crushed cardamom seeds, freshly grated nutmeg or seeds from a vanilla pod.

Raspberry Risotto with Glazed Raspberries

Why shouldn't risotto be served as a dessert? If you think about it,
most risottos are really savoury rice puddings. This is really delicious – try it.

Serves 4–6

INGREDIENTS

450 ml/16 fl oz/2 cups milk
450 ml/16 fl oz/2 cups canned
   unsweetened coconut milk
pinch of salt
1 vanilla pod, split
2–3 strips lemon rind
25 g/1 oz/2 tbsp unsalted butter

125 g/4$^{1}/_{2}$ oz/$^{2}/_{3}$ cup arborio rice
50 ml/2 fl oz/$^{1}/_{4}$ cup dry white
   vermouth
100 g/3$^{1}/_{2}$ oz/$^{1}/_{2}$ cup sugar
120 ml/4 fl oz/$^{1}/_{2}$ cup double (heavy)
   or whipping cream
2–3 tbsp raspberry-flavoured liqueur

350 g/12 oz/about 2 cups fresh
   raspberries
2 tbsp good-quality raspberry jam or
   preserve
squeeze of lemon juice
toasted flaked (slivered) almonds,
   to decorate (optional)

1 Heat the milk in a heavy-based saucepan with the coconut milk, salt, vanilla pod and lemon rind until bubbles begin to form around the edge of the pan. Reduce the heat to low and keep the milk mixture hot, stirring occasionally.

2 Heat the butter in another large heavy-based pan over a medium heat until foaming. Add the rice and cook, stirring, for 2 minutes to coat well.

3 Add the vermouth; it will bubble and steam rapidly. Cook, stirring, until the wine is completely absorbed. Gradually add the hot milk, about 120 ml/4 fl oz/½ cup at a time, allowing each addition to be absorbed completely before adding the next.

4 When half the milk has been added, stir in the sugar until dissolved. Continue stirring and adding the milk until the rice is tender, but still firm to the bite:

this should take about 25 minutes. Remove from the heat; remove the vanilla pod and lemon strips. Stir in half the cream, the liqueur and half the fresh raspberries; cover.

5 Heat the raspberry jam with the lemon juice and 1–2 tablespoons water, stirring until smooth. Remove from heat, add the remaining raspberries and mix. Stir the remaining cream into the risotto and serve with the glazed raspberries. Decorate if wished.

Snowdon Pudding

This old-fashioned British steamed pudding was named after the Welsh mountain, Snowdon.
The story goes it was served to tired hungry climbers at the hotel at the foot of Mount Snowdon.

Serves 6

INGREDIENTS

butter, for greasing
115 g/4 oz/³/₄ cup raisins
25 g/1 oz/2 tbsp chopped angelica
115 g/4 oz/2 cups fresh white
   breadcrumbs
25 g/1 oz/2 tbsp rice flour
pinch of salt

125 g/4 oz/1 cup plus 2 tbsp
   shredded suet
25 g/1 oz/2 tbsp light brown sugar
grated rind of 1 large lemon
2 eggs
80 g/3 oz/¹/₃ cup marmalade
3–4 tsp milk

LEMON SAUCE:
1 tbsp cornflour (cornstarch)
250 ml/9 fl oz/1 cup plus 2 tbsp milk
grated rind and juice of 2 lemons
3 tbsp golden or corn syrup

1 Sprinkle a well-buttered 1.2 litre/2 pint/5 cup pudding basin with a tablespoon of the raisins and the angelica.

2 Put the remaining raisins in a bowl with the breadcrumbs, rice flour, salt, suet, sugar and lemon rind and toss to combine. Make a well in the centre.

3 Beat the eggs and marmalade for about 1 minute until beginning to lighten. Beat in 3

tablespoons of the milk; pour into the well. Gently stir into the dry ingredients to form a soft dough. Add more milk if necessary. Spoon into the prepared pudding basin.

4 Butter a sheet of baking parchment and make a pleat along the centre. Cover the basin loosely with the paper, buttered-side down; secure with string.

5 Stand the pudding basin on a wire rack in a large pan. Fill

with enough boiling water to come three quarters of the way up the side of the basin. Cover and steam gently over low heat for about 2 hours until the top is risen. Top up with boiling water when needed.

6 To make the lemon sauce, mix the cornflour (cornstarch) with about 3 tablespoons of milk to form a paste. Bring the remaining milk and the lemon rind to the simmer, then whisk into the paste until blended. Return the mixture to the pan and simmer gently for about 3 minutes, whisking, until smooth. Sir in the lemon juice and syrup. Pour into a jug; keep warm.

7 Remove the pudding from the pan, remove the paper and allow the pudding to shrink slightly before unmoulding. Serve hot with the lemon sauce.

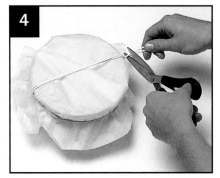

Florentine Rice Pudding

*This very sophisticated rice pudding from Florence is like a cross between
a mousse and a soufflé, and is best served warm.*

Serves 6

INGREDIENTS

150 g/5½ oz/¾ cup long-grain white
   rice or Italian arborio rice
pinch of salt
1 litre/1¾ pints/4 cups milk
5 eggs

400 g/14 oz/2 cups sugar or 450 g/
   1 lb/2 cups honey, or a mixture
115 g/4 oz/8 tbsp butter, melted
   and cooled
2 tbsp orange flower water or 4 tbsp
   orange-flavoured liqueur

225 g/8 oz diced candied orange peel
225 g/8 oz/about 1 cup orange
   marmalade
2–3 tablespoons water
icing (confectioners') sugar, for dusting

1 Put the rice and salt in a large heavy-bottomed saucepan. Add the milk and bring to the boil, stirring occasionally. Reduce the heat to low and simmer gently for about 25 minutes until the rice is tender and creamy. Remove from the heat.

2 Pass the cooked rice through a food mill into a large bowl. Alternatively, process in a food processor for about 30 seconds until smooth. Set aside. Stir from time to time to prevent a skin forming.

3 Meanwhile, using an electric mixer, beat the eggs with the sugar in a large bowl for about 4 minutes until very light and creamy. Gently fold into the rice with the melted butter. Stir in half the orange flower water, then stir in the candied orange peel.

4 Turn into a well-buttered 2 litre/3½ pint /8 cup soufflé dish or charlotte mould. Place the dish in a roasting tin (pan) and pour in enough boiling water to come 4 cm/ 1½ inches up the side of the dish.

5 Bake in a preheated oven at 180°C/350°F/Gas Mark 4 for about 25 minutes until puffed and lightly set. Transfer the dish to a wire rack to cool slightly.

6 Heat the marmalade with the water, stirring until dissolved and smooth. Stir in the remaining orange flower water and pour into a sauceboat. Dust the top of the pudding with the icing (confectioners') sugar and serve warm with the marmalade sauce.

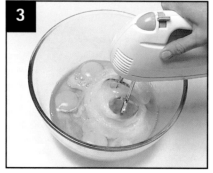

Almond Rice Custard

This traditional Turkish sweet is simply an almond milk thickened with ground rice.
Serve with the traditional decoration of pistachios and pomegranate seeds if they are in season.

Serves 6

INGREDIENTS

80 g/3 oz/³⁄₄ cup whole blanched
   almonds
1 litre/l³⁄₄ pints/4 cups milk
25 g/1 oz/scant ¹⁄₄ cup rice flour
pinch of salt

60 g/2 oz/¹⁄₄ cup sugar
¹⁄₂ tsp almond essence (extract) or
   1 tbsp almond-flavour liqueur
toasted flaked (slivered) almonds, to
   decorate

TO SERVE (OPTIONAL):
350 g/12 oz fresh strawberries, sliced,
   sprinkled with 2 tbsp sugar and
   chilled

1 Put the almonds in a food processor and process until a thick paste forms. Bring 225 ml/8 fl oz/1 cup of the milk to the boil. Gradually pour into the almond paste, with the machine running, until the mixture is smooth. Leave to stand for about 10 minutes.

2 Combine the rice flour, salt and sugar in a large bowl, then stir in about 4–5 tablespoons of the milk to form a smooth paste.

3 Bring the remaining milk to the boil in a heavy-based saucepan. Pour the hot milk into the rice flour paste and stir constantly, then return the mixture to the saucepan and bring to the boil. Reduce the heat and simmer for about 10 minutes until smooth and thickened. Remove from the heat.

4 Strain the almond milk through a very fine sieve (strainer) into the simmering rice custard, pressing through the almonds with the back of a spoon. Return to the heat and simmer for a further 7–10 minutes or until it becomes thick.

5 Remove from the heat and stir in the almond essence (extract). Cool slightly, stirring, then pour into individual bowls. Sprinkle with the almonds and serve with the strawberries, if wished. Chill to serve later, if preferred – the custard will thicken as it cools.

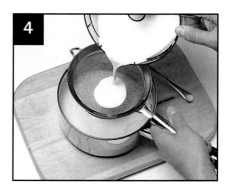

Black Rice Pudding with Mango Salad

*This sticky black rice is like congee, the traditional rice porridge eaten all over South-East Asia
for breakfast or as a base for other dishes. Delicious with a mango salad.*

Serves 6–8

INGREDIENTS

300 g/10½ oz/1½ cups black
    glutinous rice
850 ml/1½ pints/3¾ cups boiling
    water
1 vanilla pod, split, black seeds
    removed and reserved

225 g/8 oz/1 cup light brown sugar
50 g/2 oz packet coconut powder
400 ml/14 fl oz can thick coconut milk
2 ripe mangoes
6 passion fruit

TO DECORATE:
shredded fresh coconut (optional)
fresh mint leaves, to decorate

1 Put the rice in a large heavy-based saucepan and pour over the boiling water. Add the vanilla pod and seeds to the pan. Return to the boil, stirring once or twice. Reduce the heat to low and simmer, covered, for about 25 minutes until the rice is tender and the liquid almost absorbed; do not uncover during cooking.

2 Remove from the heat and stir in the sugar, coconut powder and half the coconut milk. Stir until the sugar is dissolved.

Cover and stand for 10 minutes. If the rice becomes too thick, add a little more of the coconut milk or a little milk or water.

3 Cut each mango lengthways along each side of the large stone to remove the flesh. Peel the mangoes, thinly slice and arrange on a serving plate.

4 Cut the passion fruit crossways in half and scoop out the pulp and juice; spoon over the mango slices. Decorate

with shredded coconut, if wished, and a few mint leaves.

5 Spoon the warm pudding into wide shallow bowls and decorate with shredded coconut and mint leaves. Drizzle some of the remaining coconut milk around the edges, if wished. Serve with the mango salad.

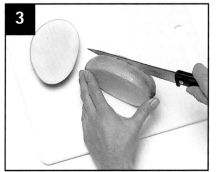

Rice Pudding Tartlets

*These delicious little tartlets have a soft dark chocolate layer, covered with creamy rice pudding –
they make a scrumptious special occasion dessert or tea-time treat.*

Makes 6–8 tartlets

INGREDIENTS

1 quantity Shortcrust Pastry (see page 150)
1 litre/1³/₄ pints/4 cups milk
pinch of salt
1 vanilla pod, split, seeds removed and reserved

100 g/3¹/₂ oz/¹/₂ cup arborio or long-grain white rice
1 tbsp cornflour (cornstarch)
2 tbsp sugar
cocoa powder, to dust
melted chocolate, to decorate

CHOCOLATE GANACHE:
200 ml/7 fl oz/³/₄ cup double (heavy) cream
1 tbsp light corn syrup
175 g/6 oz bitter-sweet or semi-sweet chocolate, chopped
1 tbsp unsalted butter

1 Make the pastry shells following Steps 1–4 on page 150, increasing the sugar to 2 tablespoons. After removing the beans in Step 4, bake for 5–7 minutes longer until the pastry (piecrust) is crisp. Transfer the tartlets to a wire rack to cool.

2 To make the chocolate ganache, bring the double (heavy) cream and corn syrup to the boil. Remove from the heat and immediately stir in the chopped chocolate; stir until melted and smooth. Beat in the butter. Spoon a 2.5 cm/1 inch thick layer into each tartlet. Set aside.

3 Bring the milk and salt to the boil in a saucepan. Sprinkle in the rice and return to the boil. Add the vanilla seeds and pod. Reduce the heat and simmer until the rice is tender and the milk creamy.

4 Blend the cornflour (cornstarch) and sugar in a small bowl and add about 2 tablespoons water to make a paste. Stir in a few spoonfuls of the rice mixture, then stir the cornflour mixture into the rice. Bring to the boil and cook for about 1 minute until thickened. Cool the pan in iced water, stirring until thick.

5 Spoon into the tartlets, filling each to the brim. Leave to set at room temperature. To serve, dust with cocoa powder and pipe or drizzle with melted chocolate.

Riz à l'Impératrice

This rich moulded rice pudding is a classic French dessert. Serve with a sauce made by poaching dried apricots in water with apricot jam and lemon juice to taste, then processing until smooth.

Serves 6–8

INGREDIENTS

120 ml/4 fl oz/$\frac{1}{2}$ cup kirsch or other favourite liqueur
115 g/4 oz candied or dried fruits, such as dried sour cherries, dried cranberries or blueberries, raisins or candied peel
100 g/3$\frac{1}{2}$ oz/$\frac{1}{2}$ cup long-grain white rice

pinch of salt
700 ml/1$\frac{1}{4}$ pints/3 cups milk
60 g/2 oz/$\frac{1}{4}$ cup caster (superfine) sugar
1 vanilla pod, split open, seeds scraped out and reserved
1 sachet (envelope) unflavoured powdered gelatine
50 ml/2 fl oz/$\frac{1}{4}$ cup cold water

2 egg yolks, lightly beaten
225 ml/8 fl oz/1 cup double (heavy) cream, whipped until soft peaks form
4 tbsp apricot jam or preserve
glacé cherries, to decorate

1 Combine 2–3 tablespoons of the kirsch with the candied or dried fruits and set aside.

2 Bring a saucepan of water to the boil. Sprinkle in the rice and add the salt; simmer gently for 15–20 minutes until the rice is just tender. Drain, rinse and drain again.

3 Bring the milk and sugar to the boil in a large non-stick saucepan. Add the vanilla seeds and pod and stir in the rice. Reduce the heat to low and simmer, covered, until the rice is very tender and the milk reduced by about a third. Remove from the heat and discard the vanilla pod.

4 Soften the gelatine in the water, then heat gently to dissolve.

5 Add about 2 tablespoons of the hot rice to the egg yolks and whisk to blend, then beat into the rice with the dissolved gelatine. until the mixture thickens slightly. Pour into a large mixing bowl. Place the bowl in a roasting tin (pan) half-filled with iced water and stir until beginning to set.

6 Fold in the soaked fruits and cream. Stir until it begins to set again, then immediately pour into a rinsed 1.2–1.5 litre/2–2$\frac{3}{4}$ pint/5–6$\frac{1}{4}$ cup mould. Smooth the surface, cover and chill for at least 2 hours or overnight.

7 Unmould the rice on to a serving plate. Heat the jam with the remaining kirsch and 2 tablespoons water to make a smooth glaze. Brush over the top of the unmoulded rice. Decorate the dessert with cherries and stand for 15 minutes before serving.

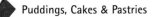

Chocolate Rice Dessert

What could be more delicious than creamy tender rice cooked in a rich chocolate sauce?
This dessert is almost like a dense chocolate mousse.

Serves 8–10

INGREDIENTS

100 g/3¹/₂ oz/¹/₂ cup long-grain white
   rice
pinch of salt
600 ml/1 pint/2 ¹/₂ cups milk
100 g/3¹/₂ oz/¹/₂ cup sugar

200 g/7 oz bitter-sweet or semi-sweet
   chocolate, chopped
60 g/2 oz/4 tbsp butter, diced
1 tsp vanilla essence (extract)
2 tbsp brandy or Cognac

175 ml/6 fl oz/³/₄ cup double (heavy)
   cream
whipped cream, for piping (optional)
chocolate curls, to decorate (optional)

1 Bring a saucepan of water to the boil. Sprinkle in the rice and add the salt; reduce the heat and simmer gently for 15–20 minutes until the rice is just tender. Drain, rinse and drain again.

2 Heat the milk and the sugar in a large heavy-based saucepan over a medium heat until the sugar dissolves, stirring frequently. Add the chocolate and butter and stir until melted and smooth.

3 Stir in the cooked rice and reduce the heat to low. Cover and simmer, stirring occasionally, for 30 minutes until the milk is absorbed and the mixture thickened. Stir in the vanilla extract and brandy. Remove from the heat and allow to cool to room temperature.

4 Using an electric mixer, beat the cream until soft peaks form. Stir one heaped spoonful of the cream into the chocolate rice mixture to lighten it; then fold in the remaining cream.

5 Spoon into glass serving dishes, cover and chill for about 2 hours. If wished, decorate with piped whipped cream and top with chocolate curls. Serve cold.

VARIATION

To mould the chocolate rice, soften 1 sachet (envelope) gelatine in about 50 ml/2 fl oz/¹/₄ cup cold water and heat gently until dissolved. Stir into the chocolate just before folding in the cream. Pour into a rinsed mould, allow to set, then unmould.

Orange-scented Rice Pudding

This delicious creamy pudding is flavoured with fresh oranges,
orange-flavoured liqueur and two kinds of ginger for a wonderfully scented result.

Serves 6

INGREDIENTS

140 g/5 oz/³/₄ cup pudding rice
225 ml/8 fl oz/1 cup freshly squeezed
   orange juice
pinch of salt
500 ml/18 fl oz/2¹/₄ cups milk
1 vanilla pod, split

5 cm/2 inch piece fresh ginger root,
   peeled and gently bruised
200 g/7 oz/1 cup sugar
50 ml/2 fl oz/¹/₄ cup double (heavy)
   cream
4 tbsp orange-flavoured liqueur

2 tbsp butter
4–6 seedless oranges
2 pieces stem ginger, sliced thinly, plus
   2 tbsp ginger syrup from the jar
ground ginger, for dusting

1 Put the rice in a large heavy-based saucepan with the orange juice and salt. Bring to the boil, skimming off any foam. Reduce the heat to low and simmer gently for about 10 minutes, stirring occasionally, until the juice is absorbed.

2 Gradually stir in the milk, add the vanilla pod and ginger root and continue to simmer for about 30 minutes, stirring frequently, until the milk is absorbed and the rice is very tender. Remove from the heat; remove the vanilla pod and ginger root.

3 Stir in half the sugar, half the cream, the orange liqueur and the butter until the sugar is dissolved and the butter is melted. Allow to cool, stir in the remaining cream and pour into a serving bowl. Leave, covered, at room temperature.

4 Pare the rind from the oranges and reserve. Working over a bowl to catch the juices, remove the pith from all the oranges. Cut out the segments and drop into the bowl. Stir in the stem ginger and syrup. Chill.

5 Cut the pared orange rind into thin strips and blanch for 1 minute. Drain and rinse. Bring 225 ml/8 fl oz/1 cup of water to the boil with the remaining sugar. Add the rind strips and simmer gently until the syrup is reduced by half. Cool.

6 Serve the pudding with the chilled oranges and top with the caramelized orange rind strips.

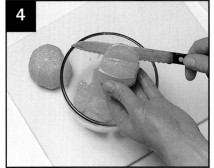

Kesari Kheer

This is a classic Indian milk pudding, full of exotic spices. This version contains saffron which gives it a lovely deep-yellow colour. The cream is not authentic, but does lighten the texture.

Serves 4–6

INGREDIENTS

25 g/1 oz/2 tbsp clarified butter or ghee
80 g/3 oz/¹/₃ cup basmati rice, washed and well drained
1.5 litres/2³/₄ pints/6¹/₄ cups milk
115 g/4 oz/¹/₂ cup sugar or to taste

10–12 green cardamom pods, crushed to remove the black seeds (pods discarded)
70 g/2¹/₂ oz/¹/₂ cup sultanas (golden raisins) or raisins
large pinch saffron threads, about ¹/₂ tsp, soaked in 2–3 tbsp milk

60 g/2 oz/¹/₂ cup green pistachios, lightly toasted
150 ml/5 fl oz/²/₃ cup double (heavy) cream, whipped (optional)
ground cinnamon, for dusting
edible silver foil (vark), to decorate (optional)

1 Melt the butter in a large, heavy-based saucepan over a medium heat. Pour in the rice and cook, stirring almost constantly, for about 6 minutes until the rice grains are translucent and a deep golden brown.

2 Pour in the milk and over a high heat bring to the boil. Reduce the heat to medium-high and simmer for about 30 minutes, stirring occasionally, until the milk has reduced by about half.

3 Add the sugar, cardamom seeds and sultanas (golden raisins) and cook for about 20 minutes until reduced and thick. Stir in the saffron-milk mixture and simmer over a low heat until as thick as possible, stirring almost constantly. Remove from the heat and stir in half the pistachios.

4 Place the saucepan in a larger pan of iced water and stir until cool. If using, stir in the cream, then spoon into a serving bowl and chill.

5 To serve, dust the top of the pudding with ground cinnamon. Sprinkle with the remaining pistachios and, if using, decorate with pieces of the silver foil (vark).

COOK'S TIP

The edible silver foil (vark) is available in some Asian or Indian supermarkets or speciality stores.

Lebanese Almond Rice Pudding

This delicate rice cream pudding is flavoured with almonds and rosewater.
If pomegranates are in season, decorate with the gorgeous pink seeds for a stunning effect.

Serves 6

INGREDIENTS

40 g/1½ oz/¼ cup rice flour
pinch of salt
700 ml/1¼ pints/3 cups milk

60 g/2 oz/¼ cup caster (superfine)
   sugar
80 g/3 oz/¾ cup ground almonds
1 tbsp rosewater

TO DECORATE:
2 tbsp chopped pistachios or toasted
   flaked (slivered) almonds
pomegranate seeds (optional)
washed rose petals (optional)

1 Put the rice flour in a bowl, stir in the salt and make a well in the centre.

2 Pour in about 50 ml/2 fl oz/¼ cup of the milk and whisk to form a smooth paste.

3 Bring the remaining milk to the boil in a heavy-based saucepan. Whisk in the rice flour paste and the sugar and cook, stirring continuously, until the mixture thickens and bubbles. Reduce the heat and simmer gently for 5 minutes.

4 Whisk in the ground almonds until the pudding is smooth and thickened, then remove from the heat to cool slightly. Stir in the rosewater and cool completely, stirring occasionally.

5 Divide the mixture between 6 glasses or pour into a serving bowl. Chill for at least 2 hours before serving.

6 To serve, sprinkle with the pistachios or almonds and pomegranate seeds, if available. Scatter with rose petals, if wished.

COOK'S TIP

For a smoother texture, this can be made without the ground almonds. Stir 2 tablespoons of cornflour into the ground rice and use a little more of the milk to make the paste. Proceed as directed, omitting the ground almonds.

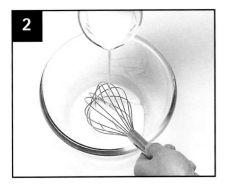

Portuguese Rice Pudding

This buttery, egg-rich rice pudding
is quite irresistible!

Serves 6–8

INGREDIENTS

200 g/7 oz/1 cup Spanish valencia,
  Italian arborio or pudding rice
pinch salt
1 lemon
450 ml/16 fl oz/2 cups milk

150 ml/5 fl oz/^{2}/$_3$ cup single
  (light) cream
1 cinnamon stick
80 g/3 oz/6 tbsp butter

140 g/5 oz/^{3}/$_4$ cup sugar (or to taste)
8 egg yolks
ground cinnamon, for dusting
thick or double (heavy) cream, to serve

1 Bring a saucepan of water to the boil. Sprinkle in the rice and salt and return to the boil; reduce the heat and simmer until just tender. Drain, rinse and drain.

2 Using a small sharp knife or swivel-bladed vegetable peeler, and working in a circular motion, try to peel the rind off the lemon in one curly piece; this makes it easier to remove later. Alternatively, peel off in strips.

3 Bring the milk and cream to a simmer over a medium heat.

Add the rice, cinnamon stick, butter and the lemon rind 'curl' or strips. Reduce the heat to low and simmer gently for about 20 minutes until thick and creamy. Remove from the heat; remove and discard the cinnamon stick and the lemon rind. Stir in the sugar until dissolved.

4 In a large bowl, beat the egg yolks until well blended. Gradually beat in the rice mixture until thick and smooth. Continue to stir frequently to prevent the eggs from curdling, until slightly

cooled, then pour into a bowl or 6–8 individual glasses. Dust with ground cinnamon and serve at room temperature.

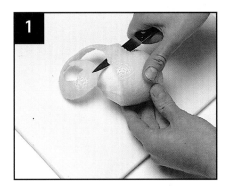

Rice Pudding Brulée

A thick creamy rice pudding with a crunchy-caramelized sugar topping. Do not refrigerate after caramelizing the puddings as the condensation will begin to wet the sugar.

Serves 6–8

INGREDIENTS

200 g/7 oz/1 cup arborio rice
pinch of salt
1 vanilla pod, split
700 ml/1¼ pints/scant 3 cups milk

200 g/7 oz/1 cup caster (superfine)
  sugar
2 egg yolks
120 ml/4 fl oz/½ cup double (heavy)
  or whipping cream

grated rind of 1 large lemon
60 g/2 oz/4 tbsp butter
2 tbsp brandy or Cognac
light brown sugar, for glazing

1 Put the rice in a large heavy-based saucepan with a pinch of salt and add enough cold water to just cover. Bring to the boil, then reduce the heat and simmer gently for about 12 minutes until the water is absorbed.

2 Scrape the seeds from the split vanilla pod into the milk. Bring to the simmer and pour over the rice. Add the sugar, and cook over a low heat, stirring, until the rice is tender and the milk thickened.

3 In a small bowl, beat the egg yolks with the cream and lemon rind. Stir in a large spoonful of the rice mixture and beat well to blend. Return the mixture to the pan and cook very gently until the pudding is thick and creamy; do not allow to boil. Stir in the butter.

4 Remove from the heat and stir in the brandy; remove the vanilla pod. Carefully spoon the mixture into 6–8 flameproof ramekins or crème brûlée pots. Allow to cool, then chill for at least 2 hours.

5 Sprinkle a very thin layer of brown sugar on top of each ramekin, to cover completely. Wipe the edge of each ramekin as the sugar may stick and burn.

6 Place the ramekins in a small roasting tin (pan) filled with about 1 cm/½ inch iced water. Place under a preheated grill (broiler), close to the heat, and grill (broil) until the sugar melts and caramelizes. Alternatively, use a small blowtorch to caramelize the sugar.

7 Cool the ramekins for 2–3 minutes before serving.

Italian Rice Ice Cream

It stands to reason that a nation which thinks of risotto as its national dish should produce a rice ice cream. Using a bought lemon curd adds extra creaminess to the chewy rice texture.

Makes about 1.2 litres/2 pints/5 cups

INGREDIENTS

100 g/3 ½ oz/½ cup short-grain
   pudding rice
500 ml/18 fl oz/2 ¼ cups milk
80 g/3 oz/⅓ cup sugar
80 g/3 oz/⅓ cup good-quality honey

½ tsp lemon essence (extract)
1 tsp vanilla essence (extract)
175 g/6 oz/¾ cup good-quality lemon
   curd

500 ml/18 fl oz/2¼ cups double
   (heavy) or whipping cream
grated rind and juice of 1 large lemon

1 Put the rice and milk in a large heavy-based saucepan and bring to a gentle simmer, stirring occasionally; do not allow to boil. Reduce the heat to low, cover and simmer very gently for about 10 minutes, stirring occasionally, until the rice is just tender and the liquid absorbed.

2 Remove from the heat and stir in the sugar, honey and vanilla and lemon essences (extracts), stirring until the sugar is dissolved. Pour into a food processor and pulse 3 or 4 times. The mixture should be thick and creamy but not completely smooth.

3 Put the lemon curd in a bowl and gradually beat in about 225 ml/8 fl oz/1 cup of the cream. Stir in the rice mixture with the lemon rind and juice until blended. Lightly whip the remaining cream until it just begins to hold its shape, then fold into the lemon-rice mixture. Chill.

4 Stir the rice mixture and pour into an ice-cream machine. Churn according to the manufacturers' instructions for 15–20 minutes. Transfer to a freezerproof container and freeze for 6–8 hours or overnight. Transfer to the refrigerator about 1 hour before serving.

COOK'S TIP

If you do not have an ice-cream machine, transfer the chilled rice mixture to a freezerproof container. Freeze for 1 hour until slightly slushy, then whisk to break up any crystals; refreeze. Repeat twice more.

Scottish Shortbread

Many recipes for shortbread contain rice flour; combined with plain (all-purpose) flour it produces a delicate crisp shortbread biscuit (cookie).

Makes 16 wedges

INGREDIENTS

225 g/8 oz/2 cups plain (all-purpose) flour
60 g/2 oz/½ cup rice flour
¼ tsp salt

175 g/6 oz/¾ cup unsalted butter, at room temperature
60 g/2 oz/¼ cup caster (superfine) sugar

25 g/1 oz/¼ cup icing (confectioners') sugar, sifted
¼ tsp vanilla essence (extract) (optional)
sugar, for sprinkling

1 Lightly grease two 20–23 cm/ 8–9 inch cake or tart tins (pans) with removable bases. Sift the plain (all-purpose) flour, rice flour and salt into a bowl; set aside.

2 Using an electric mixer, beat the butter for about 1 minute in a large bowl until creamy. Add the sugars and continue beating for 1–2 minutes until very light and fluffy. If using, beat in the vanilla.

3 Using a wooden spoon, stir the flour mixture into the butter and sugar until well blended. Turn on to a lightly floured surface and knead lightly to blend completely.

4 Divide the dough evenly between the 2 tins (pans), smoothing the surface. Using a fork, press 2 cm/¾ inch radiating lines around the edge of the dough. Lightly sprinkle the surfaces with a little sugar, then prick the surface lightly with the fork.

5 Using a sharp knife, mark each dough round into 8 wedges. Bake in a preheated oven at 120°C/250°F/Gas Mark ½ for 50–60 minutes until pale golden and crisp. Cool in the tins (pans) on a wire rack for about 5 minutes.

6 Carefully remove the side of each pan and slide the bottoms on to a heatproof surface. Using the knife marks as a guide, cut each shortbread into 8 wedges while still warm. Cool completely on the wire rack, then store in airtight containers.

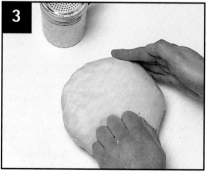

Persian Rice Crescents

These delicious little cookies made with rice flour have a fine texture and delicate flavour.
They are excellent with strong black coffee, or as an accompaniment to ice cream.

Makes about 60 crescents

INGREDIENTS

225 g/8 oz/1 cup unsalted butter, softened

115 g/4 oz/1 cup icing (confectioners') sugar, sifted

2 egg yolks

1/2–1 tsp ground cardamom or 1 tbsp rosewater

250 g/9 oz/1 1/2 cups rice flour, sifted

1 egg white, lightly beaten

60 g/2 oz/1/2 cup finely chopped pistachio nuts or almonds

1 Using an electric mixer, beat the butter until light and creamy in a large bowl for about 1 minute. On low speed, gradually add the icing (confectioners') sugar and beat for about 2 minutes until light and fluffy. Gradually add the egg yolks, beating well after each addition, then beat in the cardamom.

2 Gently stir the rice flour into the butter mixture to form a smooth soft dough. Turn on to a lightly floured surface and knead lightly several times. Turn the mixing bowl over the dough and allow to rest, about 1 hour.

3 Form heaped teaspoonfuls of the dough into balls, then form into crescent shapes. Place 5 cm/2 inches apart on greased baking (cookie) sheets. Mark a pattern on the tops with a spoon.

4 Brush each cookie with a little beaten egg white and sprinkle with the chopped nuts.

5 Bake in a preheated oven at 180°F/350°C/Gas Mark 4 for about 15 minutes until the bases begin to colour; the tops should remain very pale. Reduce the heat if the tops begin to colour.

6 Cool on the baking (cookie) sheets for about 2 minutes, then transfer the cookies to wire racks to cool completely. Dust with icing (confectioners') sugar and store in an airtight container.

COOK'S TIP

The new cooking-oil sprays are ideal for lightly greasing baking (cookie) sheets when making cookies.

Chocolate Peanut Cookies

These delicious cookies contain two popular ingredients, peanuts and chocolate;
the rice flour gives them an original twist.

Makes 50–60 cookies

INGREDIENTS

175 g/6 oz/1½ cups plain (all-purpose) flour
250 g/9 oz/1½ cups rice flour
25 g/1 oz/¼ cup unsweetened cocoa powder

1 tsp baking powder
pinch salt
130 g/4¾ oz/¾ cup white vegetable fat (shortening)
200 g/7 oz/1 cup caster (superfine) sugar

1 tsp vanilla essence (extract)
140 g/5 oz/ 1 cup raisins, chopped
115 g/4 oz/1 cup unsalted peanuts, finely chopped
175 g/6 oz bitter-sweet or semi-sweet chocolate, melted

1 Sift the flours, cocoa, baking powder and salt into a bowl, then stir to combine.

2 Using an electric mixer, beat the fat and sugar in a large bowl for about 2 minutes until very light and creamy. Beat in the vanilla. Gradually blend in the flour mixture to form a soft dough. Stir in the raisins.

3 Put the chopped peanuts in a small bowl. Pinch off walnut-size pieces of the dough and roll into balls. Drop into the peanuts and roll to coat, pressing them lightly to stick. Place the balls about 7.5 cm/3 inches apart on 2 large greased non-stick baking (cookie) sheets.

4 Using the flat bottom of a drinking glass, dipped in flour, gently flatten each ball to a round about 5 mm/¼ inch thick.

5 Bake in a preheated oven at 180°C/350°F/Gas Mark 4 for about 10 minutes until golden and lightly set; do not over bake. Cool on the sheets for about 1 minute, then, using a thin palette knife, transfer to a wire rack to cool. Continue with the remaining dough and peanuts.

6 Arrange the cooled cookies close together on the wire rack and drizzle the tops with the melted chocolate. Allow to set before transferring to an airtight container with waxed or grease-proof paper between the layers.

Christmas Rice Pancakes

These delicious pancakes are almost like little rice puddings scented with Christmas mincemeat.
They make an elegant dessert served with a custard flavoured with raisins and rum.

Makes about 24 pancakes

INGREDIENTS

700 ml/1¼ pints/scant 3 cups milk
salt
100 g/3½ oz/½ cup long-grain
   white rice
1 cinnamon stick
60 g/2 oz/¼ cup sugar

40 g/1½ oz/⅓ cup plain (all-purpose)
   flour
1 tsp baking powder
¾ tsp bicarbonate of soda (baking soda)
2 eggs, beaten
120 ml/4 fl oz/½ cup soured cream
2 tbsp dark rum

1 tsp vanilla essence (extract)
½ tsp almond essence (extract)
25 g/1 oz/2 tbsp butter, melted
350 g/12 oz homemade or bought
   mincemeat
melted butter, for frying
ground cinnamon, for dusting

1 To make the pancakes, bring the milk to the boil in a saucepan. Add a pinch of salt and sprinkle in the rice. Add the cinnamon stick and simmer gently for about 35 minutes until the rice is tender and the milk almost absorbed.

2 Remove from the heat, add the sugar and stir until dissolved. Discard the cinnamon stick and pour into a large bowl. Cool, stirring occasionally, for about 30 minutes.

3 Combine the flour, baking powder, bicarbonate of soda (baking soda) and a pinch of salt; set aside. Beat the eggs with the soured cream, rum, vanilla and almond essences (extracts) and the melted butter. Whisk the egg mixture into the rice, then stir in the flour mixture until just blended; do not over mix. Fold in the mincemeat.

4 Heat a large frying pan (skillet) or griddle, and brush with butter. Stir the batter and drop 2–3 tablespoons on to the pan. Cook for about 2 minutes until the undersides are golden and the tops covered with bubbles that burst open. Gently turn, cook for another minute. Keep warm.

5 Dust the pancakes with cinnamon and serve.

COOK'S TIP

For a Christmas custard, soak 140g/5pz/1cup raisins in boiling water. Bring 350ml/12fl oz/1 ½ cups milk to the boil. Scrape the seeds out of a vanilla pod and add to the millk with the pod. Bring back to the boil, remove from the heat, cover and stand for 10 minutes. Beat 5 eggs with sugar to taste until thick, beat in half the milk, then return the mixture to the pan and cook until thickened; do not boil. Strain the raisins, add to the custard with 2–3 tbsp dark rum. Serve chilled.

Rice Muffins with Amaretto Butter

Italian rice gives these delicate muffins an interesting texture. The amaretti biscuits (cookies) complement the flavours and add a wonderful crunchy topping.

Makes 12 muffins

INGREDIENTS

140 g/5 oz/1¼ cups plain (all-purpose) flour
1 tbsp baking powder
½ tsp bicarbonate of soda (baking soda)
½ tsp salt
1 egg

50 ml/2 fl oz/¼ cup honey
120 ml/4 fl oz/½ cup milk
2 tbsp sunflower oil
½ tsp almond essence (extract)
60 g/2 oz/1 cup cooked arborio rice
2–3 amaretti biscuits (cookies), coarsely crushed

AMARETTO BUTTER:
115 g/4 oz/8 tbsp unsalted butter, at room temperature
1 tbsp honey
1–2 tbsp Amaretto liqueur
1–2 tbsp mascarpone

1 Sift the flour, baking powder, bicarbonate of soda (baking soda) and salt into a large bowl and stir. Make a well in the centre.

2 In another bowl, beat the egg, honey, milk, oil and almond essence (extract) with an electric mixer for about 2 minutes until light and foamy. Gradually beat in the rice. Pour into the well and, using a fork, stir lightly until just combined. Do not over beat; the mixture can be slightly lumpy.

3 Spoon the batter into a lightly greased 12-cup muffin pan or two 6-cup pans. Sprinkle each with some of the amaretti crumbs and bake in a preheated oven at 200°C/400°F/ Gas Mark 6 for about 15 minutes until risen and golden; the tops should spring back lightly when pressed.

4 Cool in the pans on a wire rack for about 1 minute. Carefully remove the muffins and cool slightly.

5 To make the Amaretto butter, put the butter and honey in a small bowl and beat until creamy. Add the Amaretto and mascarpone and beat together. Spoon into a small serving bowl and serve with the warm muffins.

COOK'S TIP

Use paper liners to line the muffin pan cups to avoid sticking.

Mini Orange Rice Cakes

These mini rice cakes, fragrant with orange or sometimes lemon rind, are found in many of the bakeries and coffee shops in Florence. They are delicious with tea or coffee.

Makes about 16

INGREDIENTS

700 ml/1¼ pints/3 cups milk
pinch of salt
1 vanilla pod, split, seeds removed
    and reserved
100 g/3½ oz/½ cup arborio rice

100 g/3½ oz/½ cup sugar
25 g/1 oz/2 tbsp butter
grated rind of 2 oranges
2 eggs, separated

2 tbsp orange-flavoured liqueur or rum
1 tbsp freshly squeezed orange juice
icing (confectioners') sugar, for
    dusting
1 orange, chopped, to decorate

1 Bring the milk to the boil in a large saucepan over medium-high heat. Add the salt and vanilla pod and seeds and sprinkle in the rice. Return to the boil, stirring once or twice. Reduce the heat and simmer, stirring frequently, for about 10 minutes.

2 Add the sugar and butter and continue to simmer for about 10 minutes, stirring frequently, until thick and creamy. Pour into a bowl and stir in the orange rind; remove the vanilla pod. Cool to room temperature, stirring occasionally.

3 Beat the egg yolks with the liqueur and orange juice, then beat into the cooled rice mixture.

4 Beat the egg whites until they hold their peaks almost stiff but not too dry. Stir a spoonful into the rice mixture to lighten it, then gently fold in the remaining whites.

5 Spoon the mixture into 50 ml/ 2 fl oz/¼ cup muffin pan cups, lined with paper liners, filling to the brim. Bake in a preheated oven at 190°C/375°F/Gas Mark 5 for

about 20 minutes until golden and cooked through. Cool on a wire rack for 2 minutes, then remove the liners and cool completely. Decorate with chopped orange and dust with icing (confectioners') sugar before serving.

COOK'S TIP

Rinsing the saucepan with water before adding the milk to boil helps prevent the milk from scorching.

New Orleans Fried Rice Cakes

This classic New Orleans breakfast dish is a cross between a doughnut and a fritter.
Serve the cakes hot, sprinkled with sugar, as a snack or with a Southern-style breakfast.

Makes about 12 cakes

INGREDIENTS

100 g/3½ oz/½ cup long-grain white
 rice
1 egg
2–3 tbsp sugar

1½ tsp baking powder
½ tsp ground cinnamon
¼ tsp salt
2 tsp vanilla essence (extract)

65 g/2½ oz/9 tbsp plain (all-purpose)
 flour
vegetable oil, for frying
icing (confectioners') sugar, for dusting

1 Bring a saucepan of water to the boil. Sprinkle in the rice and return to the boil, stirring once or twice. Reduce the heat and simmer for 15–20 minutes until the rice is tender. Drain, rinse and drain again. Spread the rice on to a dry tea towel (dish cloth) to dry completely.

2 Using an electric mixer, beat the egg for about 2 minutes until light and frothy. Add the sugar, baking powder, cinnamon and salt and continue beating until well blended; beat in the vanilla. Add the flour and stir until well blended,

then gently fold in the rice. Cover the bowl with cling film (plastic wrap) and allow to rest at room temperature for about 20 minutes.

3 Meanwhile, heat about 10 cm/4 inches of oil in a deep-fat fryer to 190°F/375°C or until a cube of bread browns in about 25–30 seconds.

4 Drop rounded tablespoons of the batter into the oil, about 3 or 4 at a time. Cook for 4–5 minutes, turning gently, until puffed and golden and cooked through.

5 Using a slotted spoon, transfer to double-thickness paper towels to drain. Continue with the remaining batter; keep warm in a low oven while frying the rest. Dust the rice cakes with icing (confectioners') sugar to serve.

Italian Lemon Rice Cake

This lemony cake should have a crisp crust with a soft moist centre.
Soaking the currants in rum brings out their fruitiness.

Serves 8–10

INGREDIENTS

1 litre/1¾ pints/4 cups milk
pinch of salt
200 g/7 oz/1 cup arborio or pudding
   rice
1 vanilla pod, split, seeds removed
   and reserved
60 g/2 oz/¼ cup currants

50 ml/2 fl oz/¼ cup rum or water
2 tsp melted butter, for greasing
cornmeal or polenta, for dusting
140 g/5 oz/¾ cup sugar
grated rind of 1 large lemon
60 g/2 oz/4 tbsp butter, diced
3 eggs

2–3 tbsp lemon juice (optional)
icing (confectioners') sugar

TO SERVE:
175 g/6 oz mascarpone
2 tbsp rum
2 tbsp whipping cream

1 Bring the milk to the boil in a heavy-based saucepan. Sprinkle in the salt and rice and bring back to the boil. Add the vanilla pod and seeds to the milk. Reduce the heat and simmer, partially covered, for about 30 minutes until the rice is tender and the milk is absorbed; stir occasionally.

2 Meanwhile, bring the currants and rum to the boil in a small saucepan; set aside until the rum is absorbed.

3 Brush with butter the bottom and side of a 25 cm/10 inch cake tin (pan) with a removable bottom. Dust with 2–3 tablespoons of cornmeal to coat the evenly; shake out any excess.

4 Remove the rice from the heat and remove the vanilla pod. Stir in all but 1 tablespoon of sugar, with the lemon rind and butter, until the sugar is dissolved. Place in iced water to cool; stir in the soaked currants and remaining rum.

5 Using an electric mixer, beat the eggs for about 2 minutes until light and foamy. Gradually beat in about half the rice mixture, then stir in the rest. If using, stir in the lemon juice.

6 Pour into the prepared tin (pan) and smooth the top evenly. Sprinkle with the reserved tablespoon of sugar and bake in a preheated oven at 160°F/325°C/ Gas Mark 3 for about 40 minutes until risen and golden and slightly firm. Cool in the tin on a wire rack.

7 Remove the sides of the tin and dust the top with icing (confectioners') sugar. Transfer the cake to a serving plate. Whisk the mascarpone with the rum and cream and serve with the cake.

Sweet Risotto Cake with Muscat Berries

*Served with your favourite summer berries and a scented mascarpone cream,
this baked sweet risotto makes an unusual dessert.*

Serves 6–8

INGREDIENTS

80 g/3¼ oz/⅓ cup arborio rice
350 ml/12 fl oz/1½ cups milk
3–4 tbsp sugar
½ tsp freshly grated nutmeg
salt
185 g/6½ oz/1⅔ cups plain
   (all-purpose) flour
1½ tsp baking powder
1 tsp bicarbonate of soda (baking
   soda)
1–2 tbsp caster (superfine) sugar

1 egg175 ml/6 fl oz/¾ cup milk
120 ml/4 fl oz/½ cup soured cream or
   yogurt
1 tbsp butter, melted
2 tbsp honey
½ tsp almond essence (extract)
2 tbsp toasted flaked (slivered) almonds
2 tbsp melted butter, for greasing
icing (confectioners') sugar, for
   dusting (optional)

MUSCAT BERRIES:
450 g/1 lb mixed summer berries, such
   as strawberrries (halved),
   raspberrries and blueberries
50 ml/2 fl oz/¼ cup Muscat wine
1–2 tbsp sugar

MASCARPONE CREAM:
2 tbsp Muscat wine
1 tbsp honey
½ tsp almond essence (extract)
225 ml/8 fl oz/1 cup mascarpone

1 Put the rice, milk, sugar, nutmeg and ½ teaspoon of salt in a heavy-based saucepan. Bring to the boil, reduce the heat slightly and cook, stirring constantly, until the rice is tender and the milk almost absorbed. Cool.

2 Combine the flour, baking powder, bicarbonate of soda (baking soda), pinch of salt and the sugar. In a bowl, beat the egg, milk, soured cream, butter, honey and almond essence (extract) with an electric mixer until smooth. Gradually beat in the rice. Stir in the flour mixture and the almonds.

3 Gently spoon the mixture into a 23–25 cm/9–10 inch

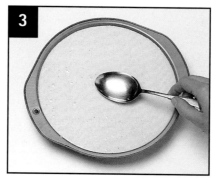

well-greased cake tin (pan) with removable bottom, smoothing the top evenly. Bake in a preheated oven at 160°C /325°F/Gas Mark 3 for about 20 minutes until golden. Cool in the tin on a wire rack.

4 Put the berries in a bowl, add the sugar and wine. To make the mascarpone cream, stir all the ingredients together and chill.

5 Remove the sides of the tin (pan) and slide the cake on to a serving plate. Dust with icing (confectioners') sugar and serve the cake warm with the Muscat berries and mascarpone cream, (pipe the cream on top of the cake, if liked).

Spicy Carrot-rice Loaf

Rice flour gives this delicious loaf a tender crumb while the cooked rice adds a chewy texture. Use any kind of cooked rice – long or round, white or brown, even wild.

Serves 8–10

INGREDIENTS

225 g/8 oz/2 cups plain (all-purpose) flour
80 g/3 oz/1/2 cup rice flour
2 tsp baking powder
1/2 tsp bicarbonate of soda (baking soda)
1/2 tsp salt
1 tsp ground cinnamon

1/2 tsp freshly ground nutmeg
1/2 tsp ground ginger
60 g/2 oz/1 cup cooked arborio or long-grain white rice
60 g/2 oz/1/2 cup chopped pecans
70 g/21/2 oz/1/2 cup sultanas (golden raisins) or raisins
3 eggs

200 g/7 oz/1 cup sugar
115 g/4 oz/1/2 cup lightly packed light brown sugar
115 g/4 oz/8 tbsp butter, melted and cooled
2 carrots, grated
icing (confectioners') sugar, for dusting

1 Lightly grease a 23 x 12.5 cm/ 9 x 5 inch loaf tin (pan). Line with non-stick baking parchment and grease; dust lightly with flour.

2 Sift the flour, rice flour, baking powder, bicarbonate of soda (baking soda), salt and spices into a bowl. Add the rice, nuts and sultanas (golden raisins) and toss well to coat. Make a well in the centre of the dry ingredients and set aside.

3 Using an electric mixer, beat the eggs for about 2 minutes until light and foaming. Add the sugars and continue beating for a further 2 minutes. Beat in the melted butter, then stir in the grated carrots until blended.

4 Pour the egg and carrot mixture into the well and, using a fork, stir until a soft batter forms; do not over mix, the batter should be slightly lumpy.

5 Pour into the prepared tin (pan) and smooth the top evenly. Bake in a preheated oven at 180°C/ 350°F/Gas Mark 4 for 1–11/4 hours until risen and golden; cover the loaf with foil if it colours too quickly.

6 Cool the loaf in the tin on a wire rack for about 10 minutes. Carefully turn out and leave to cool completely. Dust with icing (confectioners') sugar and slice thinly to serve.

Index